Canterbury in
The Great War

Canterbury in
The Great War

Stephen Wynn

Pen & Sword
MILITARY

First published in Great Britain in 2019 by
Pen & Sword Military
An imprint of
Pen & Sword Books Limited
Yorkshire - Philadelphia

ISBN 978 1 47383 4 088

A CIP catalogue record for this book is available from the British Library

Printed and bound in the UK
by TJ International, Padstow, Cornwall

Pen & Sword Books Limited incorporates the imprints of Atlas,
Archaeology, Aviation, Discovery, Family History, Fiction, History, Maritime,
Military, Military Classics, Politics, Select, Transport, True Crime, Air World,
Frontline Publishing, Leo Cooper, Remember When, Seaforth Publishing,
The Praetorian Press, Wharncliffe Local History, Wharncliffe Transport,
Wharncliffe True Crime and White Owl.

For a complete list of Pen & Sword titles please contact
PEN & SWORD BOOKS LIMITED
47 Church Street, Barnsley, South Yorkshire S70 2AS, United Kingdom
E-mail: enquiries@pen-and-sword.co.uk
Website: www.pen-and-sword.co.uk

Or
PEN AND SWORD BOOKS
1950 Lawrence Rd, Havertown, PA 19083, USA
E-mail: Uspen-and-sword@casematepublishers.com
Website: www.penandswordbooks.com

Contents

Introduction

In writing this book I have attempted to paint a picture about what life was like for the residents of Canterbury during the course of the First World War. I have done this by looking at everyday life or, rather, what passed for everyday life back then. I have looked at the efforts of those working on the home front in such areas as nursing, munitions factories and the numerous fundraising initiatives for the benefit of serving military personnel from Canterbury. It also looks at the men who left Canterbury to go off and fight in the war, and some of the acts of bravery they carried out whilst fighting for their king and country, and the effort to simply stay alive.

A book such as this would not do justice to the dedication, loyalty and the ultimate price paid by those from the city who did not make it back home to their loved ones, if it didn't include a list of those very same individuals to commemorate what they did. What makes their sacrifice even more remarkable is that the vast majority of men from Canterbury who were killed in action, or who died of their wounds, illness or disease, were not professional soldiers. These men were only serving in the army, navy or air force, because there was a war going on with an enemy who ultimately wanted to defeat them. If it wasn't for the intervention of the war, they would have still been doing the same jobs as they had done before, but life had a different destiny mapped out for them, and certainly a very different one from the one they were arguably meant to have had.

I would ask one thing of you. Remember these men, what they did and the sacrifices which they so willingly made, to enable us all to have the better tomorrow that they fought for but did not live to see. By doing so you will help ensure that the sacrifices they made were not endured in vain.

Ask yourself this, would you do the same as they did for a generation of people who wouldn't be born for fifty years or so after you had died?

CHAPTER ONE

1914 – Starting Out

With the war having started, life on the home front was already beginning to see noticeable changes in day-to-day existence. The General Manager, Mr Dent, of the South East and Chatham Railway Company, wrote a letter to the Canterbury Farmers' Club, explaining in great detail that his company's military commitments had been met in full, for the time being, which meant that deliveries of livestock, and meat traders' other merchandise, would now be handled more expediently. It had been noticed that during the period of time of restricted deliveries on non-military goods, the sale of lambs had become particularly handicapped. It wasn't just the farmers and meat companies who had been affected by the reduction in services. Hop growers, who required coal, which was an essential element used in drying their hops, had also suffered.

Never before had the Canterbury Cricket Week, in its entire history, ever taken place during such difficult circumstances. Rather than storm clouds casting a shadow over proceedings, on this occasion it was war clouds that had brought the gloom overshadowing the event. At the beginning of the week there was no war for anyone to worry about, but by the time it had drawn to a close the nation was at war with Germany. In the circumstances it was utterly remarkable that a crowd of more than 7,000 spectators turned up to watch the event get under way, but all was not well. The cricket enthusiasts were not displaying their usual carefree, light-heartedness, this had been replaced with a sense of foreboding which, in the circumstances, wasn't at all misplaced. The entire event had a slightly strange feel to it. The private tents which were usually packed to the rafters, were almost empty. For many attendees, 'Canterbury Cricket Week' had two sides to it, one was to be entertained by some scintillating cricket, whilst the other was to drink alcohol and enjoy the social side of things. The idea wasn't to get absolutely sozzled, fall asleep and miss the day's cricket on offer, but the social aspect of things, played a bit part in the event. One of the highlights of the week was the Old Stagers match, which was abandoned at the last moment. It was the first time in

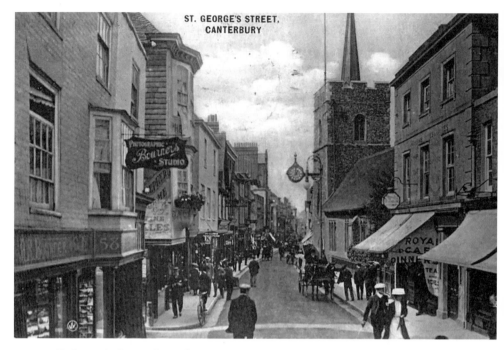

St George's Street, Canterbury.

seventy-two years of the event that it had ever been abandoned. This decision which was taken with no light heart, but was regrettably arrived at after the enforced departure of some of the 'members', being a consequence of their mobilization for military purposes.

So it was, that at five o'clock on the Monday evening after the decision had been made to abandon the rest of the week's entertainment, one of the organisers, Mr Reginald Crow, drove his car up the Dover Road with a notice displaying information about the abandonment of the week's event, as the majority of people were leaving the ground. Monies that had already been taken for seats, were refunded.

On the Monday and Tuesday evenings musical concerts took place on the Dane John, where large crowds were in attendance, as the gloom and darkness of ever-increasing war clouds appeared to have been replaced with raw, emotional, patriotism as the outbreak of war drew ever nearer. The Band of the Royal Marines were in attendance on the Monday evening, and gave a truly impressive performance, which was amazing in the circumstances. The Tuesday evening saw the Band of the Royal Marines being replaced by the Band of the 6th Dragoon Guards, the Carabiniers, who were loudly applauded for each and every one of the tunes that they played, which reached fever pitch when they played the national anthem. An interesting factor of the cancellation of the 'Canterbury Cricket Week', was that it hadn't cleared people out of the town, quite the contrary in fact, with crowds of people filling the streets late into the night as the outbreak of war drew ever nearer.

Colonel J. Vaughan, the holder of the award of the Distinguished Service Order, was the Commandant of the Cavalry School, before being selected to take charge of the 4th Cavalry Brigade, who at the time were garrisoned at Canterbury. Colonel Vaughan, had joined the 7th Hussars in March 1891. He transferred to the 10th Hussars in 1904.

Thursday, 13 August 1914 saw the Young Men's Christian Association (YMCA) in full swing, as it prepared for the large numbers of Territorials and Regular troops that either had, or would be garrisoned in and around the Canterbury area. It was the job of the South Eastern Divisional Union of the YMCA to look after soldiers in the Canterbury area. To this end they had taken over St George's Hall, in the town, to provide wholesome and pleasant recreation for soldiers and sailors during their free time. It was hoped that by having such facilities where they could read newspapers, write letters to their sweethearts and loved ones, play the piano, snooker, cards, darts or board games, in an environment of relative peace and quiet, incidents of drunkenness and disturbances would greatly reduce. Many of these young men were church-going, and God-fearing individuals, whose idea of a good time didn't involve frequenting public houses and consuming copious amounts of alcohol.

On **Sunday, 16 August 1914** and with the war not quite two weeks old, there was a memorial service held in the nave of Canterbury Cathedral, which began at an earlier time than the ordinary Sunday morning service. Some 2,000 Territorial soldiers, who were garrisoned in Canterbury, were present for the occasion, and included the East and West Kent Territorials, the Kent Cyclists, the Sussex Field Artillery, along with the Royal Army Medical Corps. There were two Territorial Bands that played, both of which jointly led the singing of a number of hymns; which included, 'Fight the good fight', 'Oh God our help in ages past', and 'Onward Christian soldiers'. An appropriate sermon was read out by Canon Stuart. The text was from, 'Be of good courage'.

In **September 1914** and with the war just a matter of weeks old, subscribers to the Red Cross were given an update about the work that was being undertaken by the Canterbury Voluntary Aid Detachment, made possible by the sums of monies raised and donated, predominantly by ordinary members of the public:

1. Materials which, when once removed from their present temporary storage location at St Augustine's College, will furnish another hospital to an acceptable degree.

2. Provide treatment for twelve wounded military personnel, who up to the present time have otherwise been totally unprovided for by the Government.
3. Training for the voluntary nurses who gained experience in nursing patients which, in turn, increased their knowledge of nursing and their efficiency. Besides this they also picked up invaluable information in the organisation and running of a stationary hospital.

The Canterbury Voluntary Aid Detachment (VAD) had through their expedient and dedicated work already managed to get their hospital up and running, and had been one of the first such hospitals to have treated sick and wounded soldiers who had been sent home to the UK from the Western Front. Because of the outstanding quality of work provided by the VAD, they were in essence able to get their hospital up and running before the Royal Army Medical Corps were in a position to look after their own wounded personnel. Once the Royal Army Medical Corps were fully up and running, the VAD were able to hand back St Augustine's College so that its pupils might return to their studies, and remove their equipment and stores so that they could be kept elsewhere. Not only the men who had received treatment at St Augustine's, but also their commanding officers, spoke in the highest terms possible of the services that had been provided by the staff of the VAD.

Surgeon-General Whitehead, speaking on behalf of the General Officer Commanding of the Eastern Command, conveyed the thanks of the military authorities for the fine assistance and valuable aid that had been provided by the men and women of No. 70 and No. 100 Voluntary Aid Detachments. He was at pains to express how much their work was appreciated by all concerned and, on behalf of all of the men whom they had looked after, thanked them for their generous and patriotic assistance.

Besides the high standard and quality of their work at the stationary hospital the VAD, via volunteer doctors, had also provided training that had qualified more than sixty men as members of the St John Ambulance. What the Surgeon-General found to be truly remarkable, was how much time, effort and work had been provided by the members of the VAD and their other helpers. Whatever their individual tasks were their efforts had been strenuous and practically none of them were paid workers. It does beg the question as to why the British authorities did not ensure the Royal Army Medical Corps were already in place to fulfil that same role, before the fighting had begun.

Tuesday, 27 October 1914 saw a somewhat unusual and slightly cryptic appeal by the Archbishop of Canterbury. The cleric was appealing for the nation to commit to a period of abstinence for the duration of the war, but what people were being asked to abstain from wasn't exactly clear. I suppose if one applies common sense to the situation, he could only be referring to drinking, smoking and fornication, as illegal substances were nowhere near as pronounced then as they are today. Here is the actual wording of his appeal:

> At this crisis in our history, I should like to make an appeal to those who care to listen. Lord Kitchener has just told us, in restrained and measured words, that if the men who are giving their services to King and country are to be fit for the great task entrusted to them, we must help them to keep clear of temptations, which are shown by every day's evidence to be perilously rife. This weighty counsel or warning comes to us at an hour when we are precluded from a soldier's activities are wondering in what way we can best carry our share of the nation's burden, what sacrifice of ease of comfort we can most usefully make, in addition to gifts of a more obvious kind. Every one of us wants to help, and in some way or other to 'spend and be sent.'
>
> Lord Kitchener's appeal seems to give a special opportunity. If those who can rightly do so, and who care sufficiently to make what would be a real and sustained act of self-denial, were to undertake to be themselves 'abstainers' during the continuance of the war, the resultant good might be much as to surprise us at all. Other countries are doing something like it. Why not we? It is not every one who can, or perhaps ought to do it, and it would be the merest impertinence were we to censure or even criticise those who prefer to stand outside an effort and to let their own free-will offering be some act of another kind. But I believe there are many who, when they have thought it over, would like to take the course I suggest. By doing so they would strengthen the hands of those soldiers, the large majority of our troops, who are manfully resisting such temptation. They would be seizing the opportunity to bear a deliberate part in the self-denial and self-discipline of the hour.

I have read the Archbishop's appeal through, word for word, quite a few times now and I still haven't seen exactly what it is he was asking people to abstain from doing. I can make an educated guess at what he is alluding to, the possibilities of which I have highlighted above, but why the Archbishop couldn't find it within himself to detail exactly what it was he was asking people to abstain from, I am at a loss to understand. If it was alcohol he was talking about, I can understand if people were going out, getting drunk and then failing to turn up for work the next day, that could affect production, which in turn could reduce output and the war effort.

A letter appeared in the pages of the *Kent & Sussex Courier*, for the edition dated **Friday, 13 November 1914**. It had been written by Lieutenant Colonel J. Egginton of the Kent Cyclist (Imperial Service) Battalion, whose headquarters were situated at 2 Castle Street, Canterbury, Kent, and it was dated 9 November 1914:

Dear Sir,

It has been brought to my notice that several applications at the local Recruiting Office to join the Kent Cyclist Battalion, have been refused on the ground that the Battalion was up to strength, and could not accept any more recruits.

I should esteem it a favour if you would kindly make it known as widely as possible that recruits are wanted for both 'The Imperial Service' and the 'Reserve Battalion' of the Kent Cyclists.

Applicants should apply personally or by letter to the above address.

St Augustine's College in Canterbury first opened its doors in 1848, initially as a missionary college of the Church of England. Over time, thousands of young men, many from humble beginnings, chose it as their place of study to acquire the high standard of education which they so desired. It wasn't only religion that was taught. Oriental languages were particularly useful, with far-off destinations in mind, where students would likely be sent to on the occasion of their graduation. They were also taught practical medical skills which would be extremely useful in some of the remote locations they might end up in.

At the time of the First World War the College had its own newspaper which was published on a monthly basis and entitled *Occasional Papers*. The **December 1914** issue included the following contribution by the College Warden:

The war has brought us our own special problem, the question whether candidates for Holy Orders ought to volunteer for military service. The question at once reveals the extraordinary character of this war. For we have but to compare it with the Crimean or the South African war to see the unsurpassed height of the moral issues at stake, and the unprecedented demands which it makes on the manhood of the British Empire. If it be viewed as a fight for our existence as an Empire, it is no less a fight for the principles of liberty and fidelity to pledged word, on which our Empire has been built. Moreover, the military services may be, I believe, a valuable preparation for the Ministry, so that the time spent on it will not be entirely lost. Nor can I share the feeling of many who have commanded our deep respect, that no candidate for Holy Orders should touch sword or gun, when such principles as I have mentioned, and the honour of women, and the lives of women and children as well as of men are at stake. We who do not oppose the prosecution of the war share the responsibility for its bloodshed, even though our hands draw no trigger.

It was obvious from his words that the subject of the war, all that it stood for, and all that it meant to the students of the college, and the ultimate decision each and every one of its students would have to make, played heavily on his own mind. He continued,

Our line has always been this; we have given no other imperatively claiming obedience. We have required those who felt it was their duty to volunteer to obtain permission of societies or bishops to whom they were already pledged. Elder students whose ordination it is unwise to postpone, others whose preparation was drawing to its close with the last examination impending, and one or two others whose circumstances were exceptional, we have discouraged. All others who wished to volunteer we have encouraged. The result is that at present twenty-one are away on military service. Others I think will join them at the end of this term.

May God grant the world soon a rightful lasting peace, and bring back our students in safety to the College the stronger for their experience.

I wonder whether the native members of our Empire will see how vital is one of the issues for which we are at war, from their own experience of the value of the pledges given by the British Government. I wonder again how far the fact that the men of India are fighting side by side with British troops, will enable us to grow in the spirit of brotherhood and overcome racial divisions. And again I wonder whether some peaceful method of meeting the aspirations and needs of a rapidly growing nation will be found to take the place of the present violent method of appeal to arms.

The Occasional Papers for the same month also included a list of those 'Augustinians' who as of December 1914, had put their religious studies temporarily to one side and were serving in His Majesty's armed forces:

- Percival **Alderson**, Lance Corporal, 4th Company, 3rd Battalion, Public School Brigade, Royal Fusilier Regiment.
- Bruce George **Beale**, Corporal Royal Army Medical Corps.
- Henry **Butcher**, Corporal Royal Army Medical Corps.
- Frederick William **Collins**, Second Lieutenant 8th Cavalry Reserve.
- Harry **Crook**, Private 'C' Company, 6th Service Battalion, The Buffs (East Kent Regiment).
- Robert Cecil **Cross**, Private Royal Army Medical Corps.
- James Ramsbotham **Davies**, Royal Naval Volunteer Reserve.
- George Edward **Garton**, Private 'C' Company, 6th Service Battalion, The Buffs (East Kent Regiment).
- George William **Hobson**, Private 'B' Company, (Grimsby) Battalion, Lincolnshire Regiment.
- Arthur Kennett **Joscelyne**, Private 'E' Company, 4th Battalion, Royal West Kent Regiment.
- John Herbert **Lawson**, Private, Royal Army Medical Corps.
- John Partridge **Makeham**, Corporal, Royal Army Medical Corps.
- George **Masters**, New Zealand Contingent.
- Ernest Hampton **Nind**, Public School Brigade, Royal Fusilier Regiment.

- Bernard Anthony **Parsons**, Private (Bristol) Battalion, Gloucestershire Regiment.
- Jasper Prescott **Phillimore**, Lieutenant 6th Battalion, The Buffs (East Kent Regiment).
- Frederick Dowson **Shield**, Trooper, Northampton Yeomanry.
- Arthur William **Taylor**, Corporal 'B' Company, 2nd (Birmingham) Battalion, Warwickshire Regiment.
- Benjamin **Vaughan**, Private, Royal Army Medical Corps.
- John Tyler **Whittle**, Lance Corporal, Royal Army Medical Corps.
- Charles Henry Cecil **Winkworth**, Private, Royal Army Medical Corps.

Out of the above named ex-students of St Augustine's College, who had already gone off to serve their country before Christmas of 1914, the following men never made it home, paying the ultimate price.

Sergeant 39273 Henry **Butcher** who was 25 years of age, was serving with the 36th Field Ambulance, Royal Army Medical Corps, when he was killed in action on Friday, 1 October 1915. He is buried at the Vermelles British Cemetery, which is situated in the Pas de Calais region of France.

Second Lieutenant Frederick William **Collins** who was 31 years of age and serving with the 1st Life Guards, when he was killed in action on Saturday, 29 April 1916. He is buried at the Longuenesse Souvenir Cemetery, St Omer, which is situated in the Pas de Calais region of France. His parents lived in Rapid Bay, South Australia.

There is a Lance Corporal (G/3908) Harry **Crook**, who served with the 6th Battalion, The Buffs, (East Kent Regiment), who was killed in action on Wednesday, 13 October 1915. He has no known grave but his name is commemorated on the Loos Memorial, in the Pas de Calais region of France.

There is a Lance Corporal (G/3907) George Edward **Garton**, who was 22 years of age who served with the 6th Battalion, The Buffs (East Kent Regiment) who was killed in action on Wednesday, 13 October 1915. He has no known grave but his name is commemorated on the Loos Memorial.

It would appear from their sequential service numbers that Harry Crook and George Garton enlisted at the same day.

I found an Arthur Kennett **Joscelyne**, but he wasn't a Private in 'E' Company, 4th Battalion, Royal West Kent Regiment, he was a 25-year-old second lieutenant serving with the 5th Battalion, Royal Berkshire Regiment when he was killed in action on 26 June 1917, and is buried at the Faubourg D'Amiens Cemetery at Arras, which is situated in the Pas de Calais region of France.

I discovered a 26-year-old George **Masters**, who was a second lieutenant (4/112A) with the New Zealand (Maori) Pioneer Corps and the Royal Flying Corps, which sounds like it could be the same person. He was killed in action on 3 April 1917, and has no known grave, although his name is commemorated on the Arras Flying Services Memorial, in the Pas de Calais region of France. He had been mentioned in despatches.

In closing it is worth mentioning the fact that George Masters is shown as having a service number by the Commonwealth of 4/112A. British officers for definite, did not have service numbers, that was only for men from the other ranks.

Jasper Prescott **Phillimore**, who was 23 years of age and lieutenant in the 6th Battalion, The Buffs (East Kent Regiment), was killed on Wednesday, 13 October 1915. Along with Harry Crook and George Garton, he is the third ex-student of the ones I have named above, who served with the 6th Battalion, The Buffs (East Kent Regiment) and who was killed on Wednesday, 13 October 1915. Unlike the other two, his body was recovered and he is buried at the Vermelles British Cemetery which is situated in the Pas de Calais region of France.

On Wednesday, 13 October 1915, 6th Battalion, The Buffs, were involved in an action at the Hohenzollern Redoubt, where they captured a gun trench and the south western face of the Hulluch Quarries, but it came at a price. The Buffs lost 191 officers and men that day.

I found a 29-year-old Frederick Dowson **Shield**, who was a second lieutenant serving with the 8th Battalion, Northamptonshire Regiment, but at the time of his death on 6 July 1916 he was serving with the regiment's 5th Battalion. He is buried at the Aveluy Communal Cemetery Extension, which is situated in the Somme region of France. If this is the same man, and it would appear that it is, sometime after enlisting as a trooper, he was commissioned as a second lieutenant.

CHAPTER TWO

1915 – Deepening Conflict

The New Year had begun and the war was still going on, despite predictions that it would 'all be over by Christmas'. It would eventually be over by Christmas, just not the one that fell in 1914. The year ahead would result in a number of major battles including, on 24 January, the sea Battle of Dogger Bank between vessels of the British Royal Navy and the Imperial German Navy; the offensive at Neuve Chappelle, which began on 10 March; Ypres which began on 22 April; Gallipoli, where Allied troops landed on 25 April, and Loos which began on 25 September, and saw the first use of poison gas by the British Army.

The first Zeppelin raid took place over Great Britain, when bombs were dropped on Great Yarmouth in Norfolk. It would also see the first use of poison gas used at Bolimov on the Vistula Front. On 26 April, Italy entered the war on the side of the Allies. The first Zeppelin raid on London took place on 31 May, which resulted in the deaths of twenty-eight civilians with a further sixty who were injured.

On 19 December 1915 Douglas Haig replaced Sir John French as the commander of the British Expeditionary Force.

Saturday, 2 January 1915 saw the swearing in of a number of new special constables at Canterbury Police Court, the Mayor, Alderman F.J. Godden, who was accompanied by Messrs. W.W. Mason and W.J. Jennings, started off by saying a thank you on behalf of himself and his fellow magistrates to the gentlemen in front of them for coming forward in such a patriotic manner to serve their community as special constables. Thankfully, Canterbury had not experienced any kind of enemy raid, from either the skies or the land, but such an event was still seen as a realistic possibility by many, especially in the early part of the war. The mayor continued, saying that he believed if such a raid did take place he was sure that every one of the men stood before him would be ready to do all in their power to act as they were instructed to do so, and serve as best they could, the interests of their neighbourhood. The fact that they were prepared and willing to serve as special constables, not knowing for certain the possible extreme demands that might be placed upon them, showed their true spirit. The mayor was quick to point out that nothing should be read into special constables being sworn in. There was no imminent threat of an invasion by German forces but, he said, it made perfect sense to 'enlist' a number of special constables just in case any such emergency did arise, as it was much better to be prepared for such events rather than not allow for their eventuality; to be prepared was half the battle. These steps were being taken, not to cause any panic amongst the civil population, but purely as a precaution. The mayor finished with the following, somewhat confusing words, 'It was within the limits of possibility that such an emergency might arise, but it was not at all within the limits of probability that it would.'

On the afternoon of **Sunday, 31 January 1915** a ceremony took place at Canterbury Cathedral which saw the Colours of the 2nd Battalion, The Buffs (East Kent Regiment), who were at the time serving on the Western Front in France, deposited in to God's safekeeping. In the absence of the 2nd Battalion, their Colours were carried by Lieutenant Kelsey and Lieutenant Ward of the regiment's 6th Battalion, who were accompanied by some thirty men under their command.

The Dean of Canterbury who awaited the party at the Warriors' Chapel, was accompanied by the Archdeacon of Maidstone, Bishop Knight and other members of the clergy from the cathedral. Colonel Eaton, the commanding officer of the 6th Battalion, formally asked the dean's acceptance of the Colours until the termination of the war, and the dean, in reply said, 'We pray to God to bring back the 2nd Battalion in safety, when they will come to reclaim their Colours.'

A service was held at the cathedral to mark the occasion, which was attended by all officers and soldiers who were serving with the 6th Battalion.

On **Tuesday, 2 March 1915** a man appeared before the magistrates at the Canterbury Police Court. The Bench consisted of the Mayor, Alderman Godden, Mr T. Wacher and Alderman Gentry. The man before them, Edward Berry, was a 21-year-old private with the 7th Battalion, King's Liverpool Regiment, who was quartered at Canterbury's Polo Club. The charge he faced was that of unlawful wounding with the intent to cause grievous bodily harm, to one Albert Slingsby, a private in the 3rd Dragoon Guards.

Chief Constable Dain said it appeared that Slingsby and a friend named Kelly entered a 'refreshment' house (café) in Palace Street, on Saturday night to have some supper. Upon leaving they were accosted by a soldier of the 7th Battalion, King's Liverpool Regiment, who called out to them to stop. Slingsby by now had the distraction of talking to a woman by the name of Cornfield, and wasn't really paying too much attention to anything else. Berry, and three of his colleagues from the same regiment, approached Slingsby and enquired if he had earlier been at the Falstaff Inn. Slingsby replied that he hadn't, being more interested in continuing the conversation with the woman.

Berry, continuing with his questions, asked Slingsby if he was with the Royal Field Artillery, to which he replied that he was with the Dragoon Guards. Not satisfied with the answer Berry accused Slingsby of being one of those responsible for injuring his left arm, which was heavily bandaged. Before Slingsby could respond, Berry rushed at him, stabbing him in the chest, causing Slingsby to stumble slightly, more in shock than anything else, before calling out, 'You have stabbed me' and saw Berry holding a clasp knife in his right hand. He undid his khaki tunic and it was clear that he was bleeding heavily. Berry and the three others ran off, and Slingsby and Kelly gave chase, but it was not long before Slingsby collapsed to the pavement due to a loss of blood. Undeterred, Kelly continued the chase and managed to catch up with Berry, hold on to him and hand him over to the Military Police.

Slingsby was taken to the Kent and Canterbury Hospital, where he was found to have an inch-deep wound in his chest, and the doctor who examined him said that the wound could have been inflicted by the type of knife which Berry was in possession of when he was detained, remembering of course that this was a day and age before the breakthrough of DNA and forensics. When charged with the offence, Berry replied that he couldn't remember anything about the incident as he was 'boosey' at the time.

The chief constable handed the members of the Bench, two army clasp knives for them to examine in close detail, one of which had blood on the point of the marlin spike, whilst informing them that he only intended to produce sufficient evidence to justify having Berry remanded in custody.

The evidence of Elizabeth Kate Cornfield was heard next. She lived with her parents at 56 King Street, Canterbury, and worked at the refreshment rooms at 14 Palace Street. She told the court that at about 9.30 pm on the Sunday night, Private Slingsby entered the refreshment rooms with another soldier, whom he said was his step-brother. They ordered their food, ate it and got up to leave at about 9.50 pm, just as the man she now knew to be Berry entered the premises. Berry and Slingsby had a brief conversation and Berry then left, but returned a short time later with three other men, at which time she was standing outside talking with Slingsby. The four men approached them and Berry asked if he was one of the soldiers who had been 'cutting them about with knifes in North Lane' and if he belonged to the Royal Field Artillery. Slingsby replied that he wasn't, but Berry repeated the question. Miss Cornfield described how she saw Berry holding an open knife which he then raised in his right hand before stabbing Slingsby on the right side of his chest. Shen then described seeing blood spurting out of the wound after Slingsby had undone his tunic to look at the wound. The case was then adjourned for a week.

On **Monday, 22 March 1915** Private Edward Berry was charged, whilst on remand, with maliciously wounding Private Albert Slingsby, and committed for trial at the Canterbury Quarter Sessions.

Friday, 16 April 1915 saw two aircraft pass over Canterbury. The first one flew over high up in the sky, too high to be recognised as being either British or German. The second, which passed over about twenty minutes later, was unmistakably a German aircraft, but there was no way of knowing if it was the same aircraft that had been seen earlier. Thankfully, for all those concerned on the ground, no bombs were dropped, and the machine made off at great speed in the direction of Dover. What was believed to be the same German aircraft passed over the city again, about forty-five minutes later, and was heading in the general direction of the north-east and once again, thankfully, no bombs were dropped. What was really concerning for the people on the ground though was the fact that on neither occasion was there any response by British aircraft to defend them against a potential attack.

Despite there being a war going on everybody was still expected to stick to the rules, no matter who they were or how trivial the offence they had committed might appear. A good example of this was seen when no fewer than thirteen military offenders were brought before the Canterbury Justices on **Friday, 21 May 1915**. Every one of them had committed the same offence, which was to either drive a motor vehicle or ride a motorcycle on the roads during the hours of darkness, whilst displaying a brilliant light to the front in direct contravention of the Defence of the Realm Act 1914. The whole purpose of having the restriction in place was to prevent the city from becoming a potential bombing target by undetected German aircraft on a night-time raid across the southern part of the country. How ironic was it then that the very men whose job it was to protect the civilian population against such attacks were conducting themselves in a manner that could result in such attacks actually taking place.

There was another irony in this matter which would have been quite humorous if it wasn't potentially so serious. The reason the prosecutions had come to court in the first place was that the person who had originally complained to the chief constable of Canterbury about such motoring offences in the area of Littlebourne Road, was the General Officer commanding the Canterbury area. This had resulted in the chief constable deploying a sergeant to patrol the area throughout the night, which in turn had resulted in the thirteen military personnel being summonsed to appear before the justices that day.

On **Friday, 25 June 1915** the Canterbury Police Court was once again very busy with lighting offences, but on this occasion it wasn't anything to do with motor vehicles or motorcycles, but homes where the occupants had failed to properly draw their curtains or cover their windows, and light had been emitted from their properties.

Of the nine cases before the mayor and his fellow magistrates that day, six of the individuals concerned pleaded guilty. One of these was Colonel Harry Parker of Thorndene, Barton Fields, Canterbury. The mayor told all six offenders that no warning was required in respect of this offence, and nor would there be any warnings given in the future. However, having said that, he immediately dismissed all of the cases in lieu of payment of 4s for costs by each of those concerned. In the three other cases, the individuals concerned all pleaded not guilty. Two of them were particularly interesting as they involved clergymen, proving beyond all doubt that everybody, regardless of their social standing in society, was treated exactly the same.

The Reverend William Grylls Watson of Ethelbert Road, Canterbury, was summonsed on the evidence of Special Constable Poile. Reverend Watson told the court that he felt 'sore, hurt and indignant at the charge brought against him'. His house, he said, was one of the most dimly lit in the street, whilst another residence close to his, which was a matter of common notoriety, was often lit up like a Christmas tree, but as it was used by the military nothing was done about it. Like those who had pleaded guilty to the same offence, the case against Reverend Watson was dismissed on payment of the court costs of 4s. The mayor told the reverend that the law considered the displaying of lights during the hours of darkness to be an extremely serious offence, as the potential consequences could affect the entire neighbourhood, but he gave the benefit of the doubt saying that he was in no doubt that the offence in his case was unintentional and inadvertently committed.

Reverend Alfred Robert Witt, who was a chaplain to the armed forces, lived at 10 St Augustines Road, Canterbury. He told the court that all of his windows were covered with dark curtains except for the one in his study where above the curtains was the cathedral glass, although subsequent to having committed the offence he had covered the glass with brown paper. Despite his not guilty plea, he was fined 4s for court costs.

A letter appeared in the *Whitstable Times and Herne Bay Herald* newspaper, on **Saturday, 17 July 1915** which had been sent to the editor, concerning hospitals for wounded horses:

Dear Sir,

Will you kindly allow me to make known through the columns of your newspaper the results of a collection made in this neighbourhood in aid of the Blue Cross Fund, and of the RSPCA Fund for Sick and Wounded Horses.

The collection was started in November 1914, by a "Blue Cross Day" in Canterbury, which resulted in a collection of £44 2s. This sum was sent to "Our Dumb Friends League" as a contribution to their "Blue Cross Fund." Since then the generosity of subscribers has increased that sum to £52 8s 6d, including a sum of £6 3s, which has been collected in a box outside the West Gate House.

On Whit Monday another collecting day was held, this time in Whitstable, and through the generous support of sympathisers there a further sum of £37 10s 9d was raised. Added to this a special postcard appeal has been made in the Canterbury area and the surrounding neighbourhood.

This particular appeal managed to raise £18 9s 10d from a mixture of individual people, organisations and businesses, which brought the total sum of money raised to £108 9s 1d. It was good to see that there was care and concern for the horses and mules who did so much for the war effort. Like the soldiers who rode them and relied upon them for moving vital supplies and equipment from battlefield to battlefield, many of them were wounded by bullets and bombs, and frightened witless by the continuous sound of exploding artillery shells, so it was good that they were thought of and considered passionately in their time of need. For them, a severe wound to one of their legs not treated properly didn't mean an unfortunate amputation, it meant the end of their lives.

On **Friday, 27 August 1915** the licensee of the Nunnery Tavern, Canterbury, Frederick Smith, appeared before the Mayor Doctor Bremner and other justices at the Canterbury Police Court, for the offence of unlawfully selling intoxicants to certain members of His Majesty's Forces at Canterbury on Thursday, 12 August, during a time when the tavern was due to be closed to all military personnel. Smith, who was represented by Mr A.K. Mowll, pleaded guilty, but in mitigation stated that the liquor in question was served by one of his barmaids whilst he was asleep. In view of Smith's previous good character in relation to the tavern's licence, a fine of only £2 was imposed.

The same day saw the funeral take place at Canterbury cemetery, with full military honours, of 49-year-old ex-Sergeant, Walter Rawlinson Fawcett, who had retired from The Buffs (East Kent Regiment) after having served with them for twenty-one years. Since his retirement he had been employed as a steward at the depot canteen in Canterbury, by Messrs. Young and Sons, who were military contractors from Andover. Mr Fawcett who had served with the regiment throughout the South African campaign, left a widow and two sons. One had followed him into The Buffs, along with a son-in-law who had done the same, whilst another son served with the Royal Flying Corps. The funeral cortege was preceded by the band from The Buffs depot, with bearers being supplied by the regiment's 3rd Battalion who were stationed at Dover, whilst the Lancashire Brigade, Royal Field Artillery, provided a gun carriage for Mr Fawcett's coffin to be carried on. The officers, who followed at the rear of the cortege, included Colonel Dauglish, Major Sparrow, Major Marriot, DSO, Captain Warner, and Captain Stubbs, along with a large number of non-commissioned officers and men of Mr Fawcett's old regiment. The garrison's Chaplain, Reverend R.A. Witt, officiated over the ceremony.

Thursday, 9 September 1915 saw the death of Bandsman 8348, Albert Henry Nicholson, the third son of Mr James S. Nicholson, the Bandmaster of the Royal Marines. He was killed whilst on sentry duty in the trenches in France. He was the grandson of Mr J.H. Nicholson of Canterbury, the famous flautist. Albert was educated at the Depot School and at Belmont House School, Walmer. He enlisted in the 4th Dragoon Guards at Canterbury, on 22 July 1905, when he was only 14 years of age, before receiving eighteen months of musical training at Kneller Hall, where he was deemed to be 'fair' on the violin and 'very fair' on the clarinet, before transferring to the 7th (Inniskilling) Dragoons. He remained in England until 16 September 1908. From there he went to Egypt, where he remained until 2 October 1910, before being posted to India where he was stationed for six years during which time he was transferred to the 6th Dragoons.

His brother, Sergeant Charles Thomas Nicholson, also served in the same unit. From India, the Inniskilling Dragoons were sent to France, and Albert served there for nine months without being able to return home on leave.

Sergeant Charles Thomas Nicholson who during the winter campaign suffered with frostbite, returned home and by September 1915 was serving in England. Another brother, James Victor Nicholson, was serving with the 5th Royal Irish Lancers, and had served at the front from the outbreak of the war. George Edward Nicholson, served with the Royal Garrison Artillery in Gibraltar.

A letter dated **Wednesday, 20 October 1915** and signed by the Dean of Canterbury, H. Wace, appeared in *The Times* newspaper on Thursday, 28 October and showed just how strong feelings ran in relation to the devastation that had been caused by German Zeppelins carrying out bombing raids on Great Britain, the first of which had occurred in the skies over Great Yarmouth, on the Norfolk coast, in January 1915.

Consider, if you will, how powerful and how much influence the Church and the Christian religion played in everyday British life back then. This was a time when most people, no matter if they were a labourer or a lord, went to church every Sunday, and if you didn't attend, tongues wagged and questions were asked as to the reason why.

> Sir,
>
> I acquiesce, subject to one condition, in the appeal of Sir Edward Clarke and Lord Alverstone that we should abstain from direct reprisals for the Zeppelin raids. That condition is that an authoritative statement should be made that we shall make it an indispensable condition of peace that representatives of the persons responsible for these raids should be delivered up to our Government for public execution. It would be intolerable that no vengeance should be exacted for such murderous and savage violations of human and international law, and the persons of whom public examples should be made are those who are responsible of such crimes. The military defeat and political punishment of Germany would be no adequate condemnation of these barbarities. If the laws of war accepted by Christian nations are to be maintained, some specific

and adequate sanction for them must be enforced, and victorious Governments have the power to do so by insisting on such public crimes being publicly branded by the appropriate punishment of their authors. That they should be tamely endured with merely verbal protests is to my mind, impossible. If every person responsible for a Zeppelin raid knew that he was personally liable to be hanged by the British Government on the conclusion of peace, it might perhaps give him pause.

Faithfully yours

H WACE

The Deanery, Canterbury

October 20th.

I couldn't help but feel that the letter had been written with a large slice of naivety. I'm not clear whether it was the use of Zeppelins in general that the dean found abhorrent, or because of their use against civilian targets. What his views on Gotha bombers was, I have no idea, but they undoubtedly caused as much havoc, if not more, than Zeppelins did. The dean's view was akin to a boxing match between one boxer strictly adhering to the use of the Queensbury Rules, whilst up against a street fighter, who was prepared to kick, punch, bite, gouge, scratch and pull hair.

If he was that apoplectic in relation to a Zeppelin dropping bombs, it would have been extremely interesting to hear his views on the use of rapid-firing machine-guns, flamethrowers, and mustard and chlorine gas being used along the miles of trenches that made up the Western Front across France and Belgium.

In **November 1915** it was announced that a number of men from Canterbury, and those who had specifically been old students of King's School, Canterbury had been awarded different honours for meritorious services in the field. Captain (Temporary Major) H.C. Stuart, who served with the 10th Battalion, Highland Light Infantry, was awarded the Distinguished Service Order. Lieutenant D.H. Hammonds, of the Royal Engineers, was awarded the Military Cross.

Lieutenant (Temporary Captain) P.E. Welchman 1st/2nd (North Midland) Battalion, Royal Engineers, which was part of the Territorial Force, was also awarded the Military Cross. He was a student at King's School, Canterbury between 1908 and 1911. His award was earned for conspicuous gallantry and devotion to duty at the Hohenzollern Redoubt on 14 October 1915. Throughout the night and during the following morning's misty weather conditions, he continuously worked under difficult and dangerous circumstances collecting and bringing in the wounded from in front of his own trench line. This was not the first time that Captain Welchman's name had come to the attention of his senior officers for similar acts of bravery.

The Commonwealth War Graves Commission records a 23-year-old Captain Patrick Eliot Welchman, MC, DFC, of the 2nd Battalion King's Own

2nd-Lt. A. J. T. FLEMING-SANDES, V.C.

Second Lieutenant Arthur James Terrence Fleming-Sandes VC.

Scottish Borderers, who was attached to the 99th Squadron, Royal Air Force, and who died of his wounds on Friday, 29 November 1918. He is buried at the Charmes Military Cemetery, at Essegney, which is situated in the Vosges region of France.

Temporary Second Lieutenant Arthur James Terrence Flemming-Sandes, of the 2nd Battalion, East Surrey Regiment, was awarded the Victoria Cross. He had been a pupil at King's School between 1907 and 1913, and received his commission in the early months of the war.

His Victoria Cross was for most conspicuous bravery at Hohenzollern Redoubt on 29 September 1915, when he was sent to command a company which at the time was in a very critical position. The troops on his right were retiring, and his own men, who were much shaken by continual bombing and machine-gun fire, were also beginning to retire owing to a shortage of bombs. Taking the entire situation in at a glance, he collected a few bombs, jumped on to the parapet of the trench in full view of the enemy, who at this stage were only 20 yards away, and threw the bombs towards the German trenches. He was then knocked to the ground and severely wounded by a bomb thrown from the enemy lines, but despite his injuries he struggled to his feet and continued to advance the short distance across no man's land, continuing to throw bombs as he went until he was wounded again. This most gallant of acts was inspirational to his men, who followed him in to the affray, saved the situation and won the day. Not only did he survive his wounds, and the war, but he re-enlisted in the Army during the Second World War and served between 1942 and 1944, as the Judge Advocate-General of the Sudan Defence Force.

On **Saturday, 20 November 1915** the St Augustine's Bench at Canterbury sentenced Harriet Baker of Herne Bay, the wife of a soldier, who was at the time serving at the front, to three months hard labour for neglecting her four children in a manner that was likely to cause them unnecessary suffering.

On **Thursday, 2 December 1915** a case came before the magistrates at the Canterbury City Police Court that was of a particularly nasty nature.

Walter Sothern, a burly West Lancashire Field Artilleryman, stationed at the huts, at Thanington, Canterbury, was charged with three offences: (1) Being drunk and disorderly in Watling Street, Canterbury; (2) Breaking a pane of glass, value 7s 6d; (3) Unlawfully assaulting Councillor Albert William Anderson, proprietor of the Watling Street Garage, Canterbury.

Shoeing-smith Harcourt of the 2nd/6th Battalion, Liverpool Regiment, told the court that at about 9.15 pm he was walking in to Watling Street with some of his friends and colleagues, when he saw Sothern on the ground with a chauffeur. Harcourt and some of his group intervened and managed to get Sothern off the chauffeur, and restrained him on the ground until the police arrived. Harcourt said there was another man with Sothern who just walked away, and as they hadn't actually seen him do anything they didn't go after him.

Police Constable Maple gave evidence concerning the state and condition of Sothern when he was brought in to the police station. He didn't repeat the actual language that had been used, but he described it as being obscene, and as an experienced policeman he could tell straight away that Sothern was drunk.

Albert William Anderson or, to give him his official title, Councillor Anderson, with a badly discoloured and very sore-looking right eye, stepped forward to give his evidence. He told the court how on the evening in question he was standing in the doorway of his garage office when Sothern, who was in military uniform, approached and asked who was in charge of the garage. He told him that he was the man in charge, and without saying another word or warning, Sothern punched him on the right side of his face near to his eye. Sothern then repeated the action with his left fist but the punch didn't connect, instead he broke a pane of glass in a show case. Councillor Anderson then grabbed hold of Sothern in a headlock and bent him down towards the floor. Another man, a friend of Sothern's, suddenly appeared and punched him under his rib cage on his left side, so Anderson did the same to him and grabbed him in a headlock before shouting out for assistance, which was when two of his employees came along and pulled the other man away, which was immediately followed by Sothern seizing the opportunity to kick out at Anderson.

The magistrates' clerk asked Anderson if there was any reason for the attack, to which he replied that it was a totally unprovoked attack. Sothern, who was 20 years of age, offered as his only excuse the fact that he was drunk at the time. An officer of Sothern's regiment provided the court with evidence that he was of previous bad character. He had originally been serving in the first line of the regiment, but when they were sent abroad, Sothern was left behind. He, Sothern, had been before the regiment's colonel for a similar offence which involved him having struck a superior officer. The mayor was far from impressed, and said that evidently Sothern was an undesirable individual who should at all times, but especially when he was in His Majesty's uniform, behave himself like a reasonable human being instead of continually having rows in his camp. The mayor deemed he was not fit to proceed to war as he assaulted peaceful individuals, whilst damaging their property. He obviously needed to be taught a lesson that he would hopefully learn from, and he was sent to prison for a period of six weeks. The mayor thanked Harcourt and his companions for the assistance they had given in getting Sothern in to custody.

Walter Sothern was a Driver (686011) in the 115th Brigade, Royal Field Artillery, which was a Territorial unit. Despite his disgraceful behaviour he was awarded both the British War Medal and the Victory Medal, for his wartime military service.

An interesting case appeared before the magistrates at the Canterbury City Police Court on **Saturday, 4 December 1915** which involved a 22-year-old man by the name of Cardinal, who lived at 49 Black Griffin Lane, Canterbury. He wasn't there having being summonsed in relation to a criminal offence of which he was believed responsible for, instead he was there applying for a permit to be allowed to travel to Canada to take up a position as a servant, where he expected to remain for at least two years. Cardinal had brought with him a bundle of papers to help his case. One of them showed that in September 1914 he had enlisted in the Army, but was discharged just nine days later, as it was determined that he was not likely to become an efficient soldier, due to medical reasons. Undeterred, he had then tried to enlist in the Royal Navy, but was also rejected by them, once again on medical grounds. He told the court that he had no experience of munitions or engineering work.

The Chairman of the Bench, Mr Silas Williamson, consented to sign the green form, which was the one which in essence approved his travel to Canada, but he refused to sign the white form, which would appear to have been the 'reference' part of the application, as he had no personal knowledge of Mr Cardinal.

On searching the 1911 England census, I found a Christopher Cardinal who was then 18 years of age, which would have made him 22 years of age in 1915. He was shown as being a single man, and a butcher by trade, but interestingly enough he was shown as being a patient at the Kent and Canterbury Hospital, in Longport Street, Canterbury, although there was no mention of why he had been admitted. Nor could I find any record of him ever having travelled to Canada.

There are many examples of ordinary members of the public doing their bit for the war effort on the home front. Individuals, charities and organisations alike, looked to raise money or provide items of food and clothes for wounded prisoners and their families. An example of this came in the form of a letter which appeared in the *Whitstable Times and Herne Bay Herald* dated **Saturday, 25 December**:

Will any kind friends who are interested in the sick and wounded soldiers at the Kent and Canterbury Hospital help to try and make Christmas as bright as possible for them by sending evergreens for decorations or fairy lights. Also some small gifts such as socks, mittens, scarfs, pipes, tobacco, cigarettes, matches, writing paper, envelopes, or chocolate, so that each soldier can have some small present on Christmas morning. They will also have a tea given them one evening during Christmas week and if anyone would like to send a cake, buns, potted meat, sweets, biscuits, crackers or jam, they will be most gratefully received by,

Miss Mabel Plummer
9 St. George's Place,
Canterbury

who will receive and acknowledge the gifts for the Sister of the Soldiers' Wards.

The 1911 census showed Mabel Plummer as a 37-year-old single woman who worked as a nurse, and was living at Lindsay Lodge, Westgate-on-Sea, Kent. It was an interesting fact in itself that a newspaper was actually published on Christmas Day, regardless of what its content consisted of, but with a war on, the news kept on coming thick and fast.

Mr A.R. Moore, who was an assistant master at St Dunstan's School in Canterbury, had been commissioned as a second lieutenant in the 2nd/8th West Yorkshire Regiment (Prince of Wale's Own). He had previously been a member of the Artists Officer Training Corps.

Corporal of Horse, Sergeant William George Eason, Royal Horse Guards, who was the eldest son of Mr and Mrs W. Eason of The Black Dog public house, Castle Street, Canterbury, who had previously lived at the police stations in both Lydd and Whitstable, was awarded the Order of the Cross of Saint George, which is the Russian equivalent of the Victoria Cross, for distinguished service whilst serving with the British Expeditionary Force in France. William's younger brother, Corporal Alfred Wyles Eason, also served during the First World War with the 2nd Life Guards.

As 1915 drew to a close, it had been an exhausting and costly year and although the war had moved forward, it had not really progressed that much at all. There was no real belief that the war would end anytime soon, it had now become a must-win situation no matter what the cost, both in financial terms and human life. Other than the use of tanks, there would be no real change in the tactics deployed by senior officers; artillery bombardments followed by infantry attacks on enemy trenches, fortified by barbed wire and large numbers of machine guns. Stop during the dash across no man's land, and a soldier risked being court martialled for cowardice and being shot at dawn if found guilty. The other option was to continue on, head-first towards a molten-lead-firing machine-gun position. Now that is what you could most definitely call the lesser of two evils.

CHAPTER THREE

1916 – The Realisation

I believe that without doubt the most monumental year of the war was 1916. So many things happened in this year which, for a plethora of reasons, made a lasting effect on the war and although these were matters that were at a national level, they also had a knock-on effect for the people of Canterbury.

After a disastrous campaign in Gallipoli, the evacuation of British and other Allied troops was completed on **8 January**. The Gallipoli Campaign had begun on 25 April 1915 and had lasted for eight months, two weeks and one day, before the decision was finally taken to beat a hasty retreat. Allied troops involved in what many would describe as an ill thought out decision in the first place, came from Great Britain, Australia, New Zealand, the British Raj, Newfoundland, and France. The main reason for the campaign was for the Allies to secure a shorter sea route to Russia. In part the decision for the Allied attack of the region was the brainchild of Winston Churchill who was, at the time, the First Lord of the Admiralty. The campaign, which had lasted for 222 days had resulted in 252,000 casualties, which averages out at 1,135 men for each day of the fighting.

Thursday, 2 March 1916 saw conscription come into being, by the British Government as part of the Military Service Act, for the first time in its history. Prior to this British armies had always relied on voluntary enlistment, but this new Act affected men who were between 18 and 41 years of age and made them liable to be called up unless they were married, widowed with children, serving in the Royal Navy, a minister of any religious persuasion, or working in what had been officially classed as a reserved occupation. The reason for bringing the Act in was simple, the army needed more men because more and more of them were being killed or wounded which, it could be sensibly argued, was just as much down to poor British military tactics as it was to the offensive strength and power of German forces. A second and updated version of the Act came into being in May 1916, when married men were included in those who were liable to be called up. In 1918, a third version of the Act was introduced, which extended the upper age limit of men who were liable for military service to 51.

A man, or his employer on his behalf, could apply to a local Military Service Tribunal if they felt that they had been unfairly called up for military service. These Tribunals had the power to grant exemptions to individuals from having to undertake military training. The exemptions could be conditional, temporary, or absolute, although the latter category was rarely given. For those not happy with the decisions meted out by one of these Tribunals, they had the right to appeal their case to a County Appeal Tribunal. The grounds on which an application could be appealed were that the man was engaged in work of national importance, business or domestic hardship, and those who had a conscientious objection, the latter category, usually being connected to a deeply held religious ground, although the Act simply highlighted an individual who had a conscientious objection to having to undertake military service.

On top of the County Appeal Tribunals there was also a Central Tribunal, which sat at Westminster in London and dealt with unusual or difficult cases, but this wasn't a given, where individuals had a right to have their case heard by the Central Tribunal; it sat only at the discretion of the Appeals Tribunal. Even though, at the time, Ireland was part of the United Kingdom, the Military Services Act did not extend to the region, for political reasons.

Up and down the country there were a total of 2,086 local Military Service Tribunals, which were in use most weeks, and 83 County Appeals Tribunals. An amazing statistic of the Tribunal system is that by the end of June 1916, just four months after it had come into being, 770,000 men had enlisted and joined the British Army, but during the same time period 748,587 men had applied to tribunals, to be exempt from having to undergo military training, and by October 1916 the number of men who held exemptions, or who had cases pending, had risen to 1.1 million men. This went a long way to showing the true feelings that people had about the war throughout the country.

One point that I feel needs highlighting is that very few young men had the right to vote in 1914, which left many of them feeling deeply resentful at being sent off to war by a group of politicians who they didn't even have the right to *decide* if they wanted to vote for.

The Battle of the Somme, which included soldiers from Great Britain, Ireland, Australia, New Zealand, Newfoundland, the British Raj, Canada, Bermuda, the Union of South Africa, and Southern Rhodesia, which is now Zimbabwe, up against those of the German Empire, began on **1 July** and continued on until **18 November**. British casualties on the first day alone amounted to some 50,000 men, nearly 20,000 of whom were killed. By the end of the battle Britain had lost 481,842 men, which for the 141 days of its duration meant that they lost an average of 3,417 each day. The Battle of the Somme, actually consisted of thirteen smaller battles:

- Battle of Albert, 1–13 July
- Battle of Bazentin Ridge, 1–17 July
- Battle of Fromelles, 19–20 July
- Battle of Delville Wood, 14 July–15 September
- Battle of Pozieres, 23 July–7 August
- Battle of Guillemont, 3–6 September
- Battle of Ginchy, 9 September
- Battle of Flers-Courcelette, 15–22 September
- Battle of Morval, 25–28 September
- Battle of Thiepval Ridge, 26–28 September
- Battle of the Transloy Ridges, 1 October–11 November
- Battle of the Ancre Heights, 1 October–11 November
- Battle of the Ancre, 13–18 November

There were at least four men with Canterbury connections who were killed on the first day of the Battle of the Somme. The first three of these men have no known graves, but their names are commemorated on the Thiepval Memorial, in the Somme region.

Rifleman 3899 Frederick James **Scott**, was 25 years of age and served with 'C' Company, 1st/16th Battalion, the London Regiment (Queen's Westminster Rifles). His parents, John and Annie Scott, lived at 30 St Martin's Road, Canterbury.

Lance Corporal PS/1793 Edward L. **Winterhalder**, was only 19 years of age and served with 'B' Company, 16th Battalion Middlesex Regiment. His parents, Leo and Josephine Winterhalder, lived at 9 Station Road West, Canterbury.

Second Lieutenant Charles Edward Stephen **Watson**, was 20 years of age and served with the 1st Battalion, East Lancashire Regiment before going on to the Royal Military College at Sandhurst. As an 18-year-old he had served in the Royal Naval Reserve in Simon's Town, on the south-west coast of South Africa. His parents, William and Alice Watson, lived in Cape Town. Charles' connection with the town was that he attended, Kent College, Canterbury.

The fourth of these men has no direct link with Canterbury but something he did does, so I have decided to include him as his story makes for interesting reading. Captain Wilfred Percy **Nevill**, who was also known by his nickname of 'Billie' served with the 1st Battalion, East Yorkshire Regiment, but was attached to the 'B' Company, 8th Battalion, East Surrey Regiment, who on the morning of the first day of the Battle of the Somme were in trenches near the French village of Carnoy, which is about 10 kilometres south-east of Albert.

Captain Nevill, who I can only assume had a character that had a very humorous side to it, bought four footballs whilst he was on leave in London, these were for each of the four platoons under his direct command. In other accounts there were only two footballs and not four. His master plan was that on the first day of the battle, one man from each of the four platoons would kick the footballs as far in to no man's land as they could, and the one that landed closest to the German lines would win a prize provided by Captain Nevill. Maybe conscious of the old adage, 'don't ask others to do something that you are not prepared to do yourself', or possibly because he just wanted to lead by example, he kicked the first ball. One of the footballs

Captain Wilfred Percy Nevill.

was inscribed with the following ditty. 'The Great European Cup. The Final, East Surreys v Bavarians. Kick off at Zero.'

The reason behind the kicking of the footballs is that Nevill and his fellow officers were concerned about how their men would perform when called upon to 'go over the top' on the first day of the Battle of the Somme. The hope was that the familiarity of the footballs would help the men stay calm. All be it at a heavy cost, the men of the East Surreys achieved their objective, Captain Nevill and 142 of his colleagues were killed in the effort, Nevill just a matter of yards from the German lines.

If my research is correct, two of these footballs survived. One example is held at the National Army Museum, whilst the other, and this is where the Canterbury connection comes from, was held for a time at the Queen's Regimental Museum at Howe Barracks, Canterbury. An incredible story by any stretch of the imagination, especially on such a momentous occasion.

On **7 December**, with the support of both the Conservative and Labour leaders, David Lloyd George replaced Herbert Asquith as the British prime minister. During the first couple of years of the war Lloyd George was Chancellor of the Exchequer, and in 1915 he was appointed Minister of Munitions. At the time of the Battle of Somme he became the Secretary of

State for War, before becoming prime minister on 7 December, a position he held until 19 October 1922.

At different times throughout **1916**, Germany looked to make a peace deal but David Lloyd George was having none of it. The only end to the war he could foresee was the total defeat of Germany. As early as 8 February 1916 the German Chancellor, Theobald von Bethmann-Hollweg, made a peace proposal to Britain and her allies via Pope Benedict XV. In essence, the proposal called for a return to pre-war boundaries, the only aspect open for discussion, as far as Germany was concerned, were her overseas territories. A member of the British aristocracy became heavily involved in the matter.

The 5th Marquess of Lansdowne, Henry Petty-Fitzmaurice, circulated a letter which supported a negotiated peace settlement with Germany, 'in the name of saving civilization', but it did not achieve the effect that he was obviously hoping it would as it was roundly condemned by nearly all other British statesmen. On replacing Herbert Asquith as British Prime Minister, David Lloyd George reaffirmed the British and French position stating that the only acceptable peace as far as they were concerned would be achieved through the outright and absolute defeat of Germany; and so the war continued.

At least eleven men, who died throughout the course of 1916, were either from or had connections with Canterbury, but had died whilst serving with Canadian forces.

Sergeant 57112 Cyril Herbert **Gilham,** was 26 years of age and a married man, who was serving with the 20th Battalion, Canadian Infantry (1st Central Ontario Regiment), when he died of his wounds on Wednesday, 16 February 1916. He is buried at the Boulogne Eastern Cemetery, which is situated in the Pas de Calais region of France. His parents, Arthur and Annie Gilham lived in Canterbury, whilst his wife, Eva, lived in Paris, Ontario.

Private 192481 Charles Harold **David**, was 21 years of age and serving with the 16th Battalion, Canadian Infantry (Manitoba Regiment), when he was killed in action on Wednesday, 19 April 1916. He is buried at the Woods Cemetery, which is situated in the West-Vlaanderen region of Belgium. He was the only son of Charles and Elizabeth David, who lived at 75 St Dunstan's Street, Canterbury.

Private 7821114 Albert **Gibbons**, was just 20 years of age, a single man, who died of pneumonia on Monday, 15 May 1916, whilst a member of the 128th Battalion, Canadian Infantry. He is buried at Moose Jaw Cemetery, which is situated in the Saskatchewan region of Canada. His parents, Walter and Annie Eliza Gibbons, lived at Upstreet, Canterbury.

Corporal 421034 William Douglas **Watson**, was 29 years of age, a married man and serving with the 16th Battalion, Canadian Infantry (Manitoba Regiment), when he was killed in action sometime between Monday 4 and Thursday, 7 September 1916. He is buried at the Regina Trench Cemetery, Grandcourt, in the Somme region. His parents, John and Anne Watson, lived in Canterbury, whilst his widow who had subsequently remarried by the end of the war and taken the surname of Lauritson, lived in Minnedosa, Manitona.

Private 142354 Percival Egerton **Harvey**, was 32 years of age and serving with the 58th Battalion, Canadian Infantry, when he was killed in action on Wednesday, 20 September 1916. He has no known grave, but his name is commemorated on the Vimy Memorial in the Pas de Calais region of France. His parents, Philip and Eliza Harvey, lived at 4 Union Row, St Paul's, Canterbury. Kent. He was one of four brothers who served during the war, only two of them survived.

Soldier of the East Kent Regiment.

His brother, Charles Stuart **Harvey**, had also emigrated to Canada and served with Canadian forces during the First World War. He had previously served as a private in the 4th (Territorial) Battalion, The Buffs (East Kent Regiment), and immediately prior to enlisting he had served as a police officer for two-and-a-half years. He had enlisted in the Canadian Army on 22 September 1914.

Private A/22072 Timothy **Gibbons**, was 28 years of age and serving with 'C' Company, 8th Battalion, Canadian Infantry (Manitoba Regiment), when he was killed in action on Tuesday, 26 September 1916. He is buried at the Courcelette British Cemetery, which is situated in the Somme region. His parents, Mr and Mrs Walter Gibbons, lived at Norfolk House, Upstreet, Canterbury.

Private 171355 Thorold Bruce **Parker**, was 30 years of age and serving with the 5th Canadian Mounted Rifles (Quebec Regiment), when he was killed in action sometime on either Sunday, 1 or Monday, 2 October 1916. He has no known grave, but his name is commemorated on the Vimy Memorial, which is situated in the Pas de Calais region of France. His parents, James and Sarah Parker, lived at 'Blean', Canterbury.

Private 101006 Frederick Charles **Giles**, was 26 years of age and serving with the 49th Battalion, Canadian Infantry (Alberta Regiment), when he was killed in action on Monday, 9 October 1916. He has no known grave, but his name is also commemorated on the Vimy Memorial. His parents lived at 7 York Road, Canterbury.

Gunner 301616 Fred **Epps**, was 28 years of age and serving with the 5th Brigade, Canadian Field Artillery, when he was killed in action on Friday, 13 October 1916. He is buried at the Pozieres British Cemetery in Ovillers-La-Boiselle, which is situated in the Somme region. His parents lived at St Martin's, Canterbury.

Sergeant 410160 Allan **Newport**, was 40 years of age and a married man, who was serving with the 38th Canadian Infantry (Eastern Ontario Regiment), when he died of his wounds on Thursday, 23 November 1916. He is buried at the St Sever Cemetery Extension, at Rouen, in the Seine-Maritime region of France. His father, John Edward Newport, was from Canterbury, as was his widow, Norah Newport, who lived at 40 Martyr's Field Road, Canterbury.

Sergeant 163263 William George **Osborn**, who was 34 years of age, died of his wounds on Saturday, 2 December 1916, whilst serving with the 75th Battalion, Canadian Infantry (1st Central Ontario Regiment). He is buried in the Etretat Churchyard, which is situated in the Seine-Maritime region of France. His parents, James and Elizabeth Osborn, lived in Canterbury, as did William's widow, Rhoda, whose home was at 11 Albert Place, Canterbury.

Between 1 January 1917 and 11 November 1918, the total number of men from Britain, Australia, Canada, India, New Zealand and South Africa who were killed as a result of the war continuing, was 260,131. Between 12 November 1918 and 31 December 1921, the date up to which wartime related deaths were included in official figures, a further 75,988 men from the same Allied nations, died of their wounds, illness, accidents or disease. Between 12 November 1918 and 31 December 1921, there were a total of eleven men serving with either the army, navy or RAF, from Canterbury or with connections to the town, who died of their wounds, illness or disease.

Second Lieutenant Thomas **Danes** was 40 years of age and serving with the Army Service Corps, when he died of pneumonia on Wednesday, 13 November 1918. He is buried at the Canford cemetery in Bristol. His widow, Beatrice Frances Danes, lived at 'The Pynes', Canterbury.

Lieutenant Colonel Lindsay Buchanan **Scott** was 54 years of age and serving with the 1st Battalion, North Staffordshire Regiment, but was attached to the Depot, Royal Army Ordnance Corps, when he died of pneumonia on Thursday, 14 November 1918, and was buried at the Sainte Marie Cemetery, at Le Havre, which is situated in the Seine-Maritime, France. Before the war he had lived with his wife, Sarah, at Ormdale Lodge, Elham, Canterbury. He had previously served in the South African and Sudan campaigns, and had been awarded the Order of Medijieh (Egypt) 2nd Class.

Private 87466 Charles Gilbert **Gifford** was 27 years of age and serving with the Royal Army Medical Corps as an orderly at the 11th General Hospital in Genoa, Italy, when he died of influenza on Friday, 15 November 1918. He is buried at the Staglieno Cemetery, in Genoa, Italy.   Charles was born at Wingham, Canterbury.

Sapper 199942 John Henry **Dilnot**, was 34 years of age and serving with the 7th Field Company, Royal Engineers, when he died of pneumonia on Saturday, 23 November 1918. He was buried at the Southern Cemetery, Cologne, Germany. John was a married man, whose widow Mary was, after the end of the war, living at Deal, Kent. He was a native of Canterbury.

Private L/10212 H. **Potter**, was 23 years of age and served with the 1st/5th Battalion, The Buffs (East Kent Regiment). He died of pneumonia on Friday, 31 January 1919, and was buried at the Mikra British Cemetery, in Kalamaria, Greece. His parents, Frederick and Susan Potter, lived at 'Longneck House', Waltham, Canterbury.

Lance Corporal 260002 Stanley Walter **Parry**, was 20 years of age and was serving with the 2nd/5th Battalion, The Loyal North Lancashire Regiment, when he died of his wounds on Wednesday, 5 February 1919. He is buried at the Duisans British Cemetery, in Etrun, which is situated in the Pas de Calais region of France. His parents lived in Gillingham, Kent and Stanley was originally from Canterbury, having been born in the town in 1899.

Private Albert Henry **Nicholls**, was 19 years of age and served with the 10th Battalion, Royal East Kent Yeomanry, and The Buffs, East Kent Regiment. He died on Tuesday, 18 February 1919 of appendicitis. He is buried at the Ath Communal Cemetery, in Hainaut, Belgium. His parents, Mr and Mrs W.J. Nicholls, lived at 40 Black Griffin Lane, Canterbury.

Private 3639 Sydney Cuthbert **Collingwood**, was 28 years of age and serving with the 51st Battalion, Australian Infantry, when he died of pneumonia on Saturday, 22 February 1919. He is buried at St John Churchyard, Sutton Veny in Wiltshire. Sydney was born in Blean, Canterbury.

Major Thomas William Hathway **Jones**, OBE, was 42 years of age and serving with the Indian Army as the Post Commandant in Nairobi, when he died on Monday, 7 April 1919. He had previously served with the 94th Russell's Infantry, Indian Army. His cause of death is not recorded, and he is buried in the Nakuru North Cemetery, Nairobi. His father, the late Major T.H. Jones, lived at the Cavalry Depot at Canterbury.

Officers Steward 1st Class 363191 Henry John **Stone,** was 35 years of age and was serving with the Royal Navy as part of the crew of HMS *Halcyon* when he died of phthisis on Friday, 30 May 1919. In layman's terms he died of pulmonary tuberculosis, or consumption. He is buried at the Normanston Drive Cemetery in Lowestoft, Suffolk. John was born in Canterbury.

Private 266447 Archie **Price,** was 38 years of age and serving with the 1st/1st Battalion, Kent Cyclist Battalion, when he died of enteric fever on Thursday, 11 September 1919. He is buried at the Delhi Memorial, India Gate, in India. His parents, William and Elizabeth Price, lived at 'The Yew

Trees', Blean, Canterbury, and his widow, Sarah Elizabeth Price, lived at 18 Lancaster Road, Canterbury.

Before finishing this chapter, I want to take a brief look at a few incidents which took place throughout Canterbury on the home front.

On **10 January 1916**, a case was heard at the Canterbury City Quarter Sessions, before the Recorder, Mr Frank Safford. The man before him was 43-year-old Regimental Sergeant Major Heber Drew of the Royal East Kent Mounted Rifles, who faced two charges in respect of missing army stores. Charge one, was that some time in or around the month of November 1915 at Canterbury, did steal, take and carry away a quantity of sponge to the value of £11 8s 4d, the property of His Majesty the King, and that secondly, he did at some time in or around the month of October 1915, at Canterbury did steal, take and carry away a quantity of harness, 100 linen rubbers and about 250 sponges, to the value of £26 4s 2d, also the property of his Majesty the King.

Heber Drew had served in the army for twenty-five years the day after the case began, and had been entitled to a pension for four years, but had decided to remain in the army serving his king and country. For fourteen years he had served with the 16th and 21st Lancers, had seen active service and was in possession of medals for the campaigns in Tirah and South Africa. He also held the Long Service and Good Conduct medal. His military record was exemplary and during the whole of his military service he did not have so much as a blemish against his name, or one single discipline-related offence. He was a married man with no less than eight children, and had lived in Canterbury since 1909.

In September 1915, the 1st Battalion of the Royal East Kent Mounted Rifles, who were stationed in huts on the Old Park, Canterbury, were under orders for Foreign Service and left hurriedly on 23 September. It then became necessary to clear the huts as quickly as possible to allow elements of the North Somerset Regiment to move in. Everything that was removed from the huts was placed in the Drill Hall by fatigue parties, which consisted of a corporal and twelve men from the 2nd/1st Regiment. This took four days to complete and had nothing to do with Drew. The Drill Hall was still in use on a daily basis, which meant literally hundreds of people had access to it at any one time during the course of the day, with the doors only being secured in the evening. Also in the Drill Hall were stores which were used by The Buffs, (East Kent Regiment), meaning that anyone from either regiment along with anyone else who used the Drill Hall, also potentially had access to the missing items which Sergeant Major Heber Drew, had been charged with stealing.

He had been charged on the strength of allegations made by James Todd a marine store dealer of Pound Lane, Canterbury and James Tomlin and Kingsnorth Todd, who were both in the employ of James Todd, Lance Corporal Hollis of the 3rd/1st Battalion, Royal East Kent Mounted Rifles,

Lieutenant and Quartermaster Carlisle of the 2nd/1st Battalion, Royal East Kent Mounted Rifles, and Inspector Swain of Canterbury City Police.

Drew denied ever having being to Todd's premises in Pound Lane, or ever having met Tomlin or Kingsnorth, and claimed that their evidence was simply a pack of lies to cover their own acts of skulduggery. Drew had some excellent character references in the shape of Lieutenant Colonel Edward Frewen who had known him for some fifteen years and Father Sheppard, the priest in charge of the Roman Catholic Church, who had known him for seven years.

After all the evidence had been heard, the jury retired to consider their verdict. After a brief retirement they returned and announced that they had found the accused not guilty, which was met with loud applause and congratulations by the friends and supporters of Regimental Sergeant Major Heber Drew, who left the court with his good name and character intact.

On **Wednesday, 23 February 1916** Mr A.A. Gilham of Canterbury received the sad news that his fourth son, Cyril Herbert Gilham who was a sergeant in the 20th Battalion, Canadian Infantry, had died of his wounds in a hospital at Boulogne as a result of injuries he sustained in fighting near Ypres. In recent times, not that long before he died, he had been recommended for a commission for service in the field. Sergeant Gilham had previously served in the Royal East Kent Yeomanry, and for a time before the war he had worked for Messrs. G. Mount and Sons of Canterbury, learning fruit-growing. For some years he had lived in Canada, he was a married man with a young child.

Mr and Mrs A.A. Gilham had lost a son in the Boer War and their daughter, Miss Dorothy Gilham, was a Red Cross nurse, who had recently been taken ill with typhoid whilst serving in Alexandria. She had been sent home to the UK and was being treated for her illness at a hospital in London.

Wednesday, 22 March 1916 saw the first cases under the Military Services Act brought before the Canterbury City Police Court, of young men who had failed to answer the 'call'. Three men, William Easton, who was 21 years of age and lived at 8 Rose Lane, Canterbury, Henry George Long of 10 Artillery Gardens, Canterbury, and George William Gromson, of 1 St Jacobs Place, Canterbury, were before the local justices charged with being absentees from His Majesty's Forces.

Easton's case was heard first. Chief Constable Dain told the court that these were the first cases that had been brought under the Military Services Act, which had resulted in the three men having been arrested for failing to report after receiving their papers informing them that they had been conscripted in to the army. Police Constable Holmes informed the court that he had seen Easton the previous day at 10.40 am at Mr Browning's yard in St George's Street. He asked him if he had been attested, to which Easton replied, 'No.' He admitted that he had received notices informing him that he had to attest, the second lot of papers having been sent out from the local Drill Hall at St Peter's Lane, which invited him to attend the previous Wednesday, but he had not done so as his father was ill. He said to Police Constable Holmes. 'I am the only son to keep the home going. I have three other brothers serving in the army.'

The court heard from an unnamed captain of The Buffs that notices were sent to Easton calling him up on 5 March, but he had not replied. Easton told the court that when he received the papers he thought it was a mistake because he had not joined up under the Derby Scheme (whereby those who attested promised to go to the recruiting office within 48 hours; many were accompanied there immediately. If found fit, they were sworn in and paid a signing bonus of 2s 9d. The following day they were transferred to Army Reserve B). The magistrates did not impose a fine as this was the first case of its kind that had come before them, but they ordered that Easton be handed over to the military authorities.

In the case of Long, Inspector Smith said when he saw Long at the Post Office at noon the previous day, he told him that he had attested and that he was 'waiting for them to fetch him'. Long then produced a medical certificate signed by Doctor Frank Wacher stating that he was unfit for military service. In reply to the magistrate's clerk, Long admitted that he had since been before an army doctor at the Barracks and had not been rejected.

Mr Hammond, one of the magistrates, expressed the hope that Long would be carefully examined at the Barracks because cases where men had not been properly examined had come to their notice. The Chairman of the Bench asked the army officers who were present in court, to pass on Mr Hammond's observations to the medical officers at the Barracks. The Bench ordered that Long be handed over to the military authorities present in the court, but before this was done, the Chairman of the Bench, Mr Silas Williamson, remarked that Long should be thoroughly examined and if there was anything the matter with him, then no doubt he would be rejected.

As for Gromson, his case was somewhat a curious one, as he had refused to speak and had apparently been very nervous, but Chief Constable Dain told the court that it was the belief of the police and also that of the doctor that Gromson was simply a malingerer and trying his best to avoid military service. He refused to speak but when put in a dark cell at the police station he asked for a light.

Police Constable Inge told the court that he had found Gromson in bed at his home, and he had to dress him and convey him to the police station in a taxi cab provided by his mother. Eventually after being repeatedly questioned in court, he said in a very low voice, 'I would have gone only I kept delaying it.' The Bench ordered that Gromson be handed over to the military authorities and also fined him 40s.

A comment I often use when writing such books is how during the war, everyday life or what passed for everyday life, still continued the best that it could and, unfortunately, that included people dying for non-war related reasons. On the afternoon of **Thursday, 20 April 1916** one such death saw the funeral take place of Patrol Leader Raymond William Post of the 2nd Canterbury Boy Scouts Troop, the son of Mr William and Mrs Elizabeth Post of Northgate, Canterbury. Mr Post was a gardener, and the 1911 England census records the family home as being at 14 St Radigunds Place, Canterbury.

Many members of the 2nd Canterbury Scout Troop, under the command of Scoutmaster, Mr S.E. Haynes, and Assistant Scoutmasters, Mr Greenfield and Mr Rayner, were also in attendance. The funeral was a large affair which saw many people in attendance, both local dignitaries and members of the public alike. After the coffin had been lowered into its grave, the 'Last Post' was sounded as a final mark of respect.

Mr and Mrs Post had an elder son, Reginald Henry Post, who before the war had been a motorcycle mechanic and on 27 May 1915, when he was 20 years of age, he enlisted in the Royal Naval Air Service as an Air Mechanic 1st Class (F5104). Despite the war still going on, he was discharged from the Royal Navy on 31 March 1918 having completed the period of time he had enlisted for.

On **Friday, 12 May 1916** an eagle-eyed visitor to Canterbury Cathedral noticed that high up on the western piers of the great central tower of the nave, one of the 'Colours' wasn't actually British. What they had actually spotted was the Colours of the 49th Battalion, Canadian Infantry, Canadian Expeditionary Force. These particular Colours had an interesting history. They were lovingly embroidered, with keen enthusiasm, by some 300 women in Edmonton, Alberta, and then presented to the battalion soon after their formation on 4 January 1915. The battalion wasted no time in setting the record for the quick enlistment of the men who would fill its ranks. They were up to full strength in just two weeks from the day they had been formed, but still men wanted to join in the false belief that as many men as wanted to enlist with them, could. But sadly they had to be rejected.

Even though the 49th Battalion was raised from men in and around the Edmonton area, hundreds of them turned out to be lads and young men from England who had either emigrated to Canada, or who had been living and working there at the outbreak of the war. Some of these were from Kent, a number of whom were natives of the city of Canterbury.

The battalion was inspected soon after its formation by General Sir Sam Hughes, when he declared it to be 'one of the best of a fine bunch', and reiterated this view at the Duke of Connaught's troop review at Ottawa in June 1915, the same month that the battalion landed in England at Plymouth. Once fully disembarked, they were sent to the Shorncliffe camp, their new home, where they put in some really tough training until 23 September 1915, when an armed escort under the command of Lieutenant Colonel Griesbach (who was thought of by his men as being, 'one of the best' and was loved by all who

Captain Francis Bennett-Goldney.

knew him) brought the battalion's Colours to Canterbury Cathedral where after an interesting ceremony and address by the Dean, Doctor Wace, they were handed over for safekeeping until the day arrived when the 49th Battalion returned from the fight to reclaim them once again. Within a matter of days of the ceremony, the 49th had broken camp at Shorncliffe and left 'for somewhere in France, where it gave an excellent account of itself'.

On **Thursday, 22 June 1916** the Member of Parliament for Canterbury, Captain Francis Bennett-Goldney, had made some strong criticisms in Parliament, after an air raid over Dover in January 1916. He said he was profoundly dissatisfied with the administration and the direction of the air service, and that he had no reason to retract anything he had said in Parliament or elsewhere in connection with these shortcomings.

Captain Bennett-Goldney complained that pilots had been sent to France insufficiently trained. They had also been sent up in defective flying machines, with neither a compass nor suitable maps. He had asserted how so many aircraft had been lost because of such neglect and poorly trained pilots, such was the drive by politicians and senior military personnel to get more pilots in to the skies. The fixation on having a large number of pilots trained and aircraft built was totally counter-productive if the pilots were not sufficiently trained and the aircraft were defective.

Captain Bennett-Goldney was one who cared greatly about Canterbury. He had been the town's mayor for five years between 1905 and 1910, becoming the city's Member of Parliament in the General Election of December 1910 as an Independent Unionist.

During the First World War his family home, Abbots Barton, was used as a VAD hospital. In October 1917 he joined the British Embassy in Paris as an honorary assistant military attaché. He died on 27 July 1918 from injuries sustained in a car crash. He survived the accident, but later died of his wounds in an American military hospital in Brest, and he was buried at the cemetery at Saint

Germain-en-Laye, near Paris. His name is commemorated on the Parliamentary War Memorial in Westminster Hall, and he was one of the twenty-two Members of Parliament who died during the First World War. Not so flatteringly, he is mentioned in a book entitled *The Magpie Tendency* by Audrey Bateman (1999), which talks about stolen items being found in his home after his death, including a painting which was the property of the Duke of Bedford. Other items came from the City of Canterbury Museum and Library. He was also named in the *Daily Telegraph* newspaper on 26 December 2007 as a suspect in the mysterious disappearance of the Star and Badge of the Order of St Patrick from Dublin Castle in 1907, which were Ireland's very own crown jewels, and were a gift from King William IV in 1831 to the Order of St Patrick.

On **Saturday, 15 July 1916** an interesting ceremony took place at Canterbury Cathedral, when the Union Jack from HMS *Canterbury*, which took part in the Battle of Jutland, was hung in the nave of the cathedral.

The following is taken from Admiral Sir John Jellicoe's despatch in relation to the Battle of Jutland.

HMS Canterbury.

> At 6pm "Canterbury" (Captain Percy M R Royds) which ship was in
> company with the Third Battle-cruiser Squadron, had engaged enemy
> light-cruisers which were heavily on the torpedo-boat destroyer "Shark"
> (Commander Loftus W Jones), "Acasta" (Lieutenant-Commander John
> O'Barron), and "Christopher" (Lieutenant-Commander Fairfax M Kerr);
> as a result of this engagement the "Shark" was sunk.

At 4 pm the ship's flag carried by Captain Percy Royds, who was escorted
by Lieutenant Commander C. Vacher, Engineer Commander C. Barker,
Paymaster K.S. Carpmael, Surgeon H. Burns, and twenty Blue Jackets from
HMS Canterbury, was carried up the nave from the great west door. At the
steps leading to the Choir, Captain Royds was received by the Archbishop,
the Dean of Canterbury, and other leading members of the local clergy. There
was then a short procession through the Choir and Presbytery to the High
Altar, where the Dean received the flag from Captain Royds, before placing it
reverently upon the Holy Table. After the ceremony the Dean handed the flag
back to Captain Royds, who carried it back to the nave, where it was formally
handed to the Dean and Chapter for safekeeping.

Captain Royds stepped forward, and addressing the Archbishop, said:

> I beg you in the name of the commander and officers and ship's company
> of HMS Canterbury to accept this old flag which has watched over us
> in the warm time of battle, and we shall feel highly honoured if you will
> receive it from the din and strife of war and place it in this beautiful
> sanctuary and harbour of peace.

The Archbishop on accepting the flag, said 'I accept this flag thus given to us
for safe custody and committed to the Dean and Chapter of this Cathedral.'
The Union Jack was then hoisted on a staff at the south-east end of the nave
opposite the large ensign of HMS *Kent*, which was hung there on 1 July 1916.

The ceremony was a massive affair with numerous dignitaries from
Canterbury and other Kent towns, including the mayors of Canterbury,
Folkestone and Ramsgate, and some 500 soldiers from various regiments that
were stationed in Canterbury.

In **August 1916**, Mr Charles and Mrs Maria Allen Tomkins of the
County Hotel Canterbury, the parents of 35-year-old Captain Frederick
Allen Tomkins, of the Royal Field Artillery, and who had been mentioned in
despatches, received the news that he had died of his wounds on Saturday, 15
July 1916 and was buried at the Dive Copse British Cemetery, Sailly-le-Sec,
which is situated in the Somme region.

Mrs Tomkins received a letter from their son's commanding officer,
Colonel J. Lamont, describing him as a 'real white man', a brave and gallant
soldier, and a staunch, true friend, adding, 'A great surge of sympathy goes
out towards you from us all.' Colonel Durant wrote, that from the very start

Captain Tomkins had set everyone a fine example. Instead of waiting and scheming to get a soft billet and promotion in the early days, he just joined at the bottom, and his worth was appreciated.

The 1911 England census records Frederick Allen Tomkins as being a married man, who lived with his wife Harriet Sutton Tomkins and their 7-year-old son, Frederick, at Rayham Lodge, Whitstable, where he worked as a wine merchant and a hotel manager.

The sad news of the death of 39-year-old Second Lieutenant Alfred Sunderland Leresche, who was serving with the 1st/7th Battalion, West Yorkshire Regiment (Prince of Wales's Own) reached his wife, Hilda Leresche, on **Friday, 15 September 1916** via the officially approved casualty lists that were published that day. He was killed in action whilst fighting in France on Sunday, 3 September 1916, and buried at the Serre Road Cemetery No.2, which is situated in the Somme region.

When his wife, Hilda, received the news of her husband's death, she was staying at the home of Mrs Cox at Harbledown, Canterbury. Hilda was the second daughter of Mrs H.H. Harvey, formerly of 'The Laurels', Watling Street, Canterbury.

Before the war, Alfred Leresche had been farming in South Africa, but came to England along with his wife Hilda and their two children, soon after the outbreak of the war, in order that he could join the army.

On **Saturday, 7 October 1916,** James Spencer, a deserter from the 6th Battalion, Northumberland Fusiliers, was charged with being an absentee at the St Augustine's Bench of Justices in Canterbury.

Police Sergeant Percival told the court that at about 10.30 pm the previous evening he had met Spencer in the street at bridge, when he was walking along the main road and heading in the general direction of Canterbury. Percival stopped Spencer and enquired of him where he had come from, to which Spencer replied that he didn't know. He then asked him where he was going to, and once again Spencer replied that he didn't know. Percival then asked to see his registration card, but Spencer replied that he didn't have it in his possession at that time. He was then asked if he had ever been in the army, to which he replied, 'Yes, I am a deserter, if that is what you want to hear.' He then admitted that he had deserted from the Northumberland Fusiliers six months earlier. Spencer was remanded in custody to await a military escort.

The British Army's First World War medal rolls index cards, records four men with the name James Spencer who served with the Northumberland Fusiliers. One was a Lieutenant who was killed in action on 3 November 1916, but because of his rank we can discard him. Private 3489 James H. Spencer was missing presumed dead in 1915. Another James Spencer served as a Private (50135) with the Lancaster Fusiliers, before then serving at the same rank with the Northumberland Fusiliers, during which time he had two

Distinguished Service Order.

service numbers, 93327 and 4257854, he was also awarded the General Service Medal, so I would suggest it would be unlikely to have been him.

There was a Private 265788 James Spencer, it could have been him, but the card doesn't provide any further information about him, so I cannot even confirm if he served with the regiment's 6th Battalion. It would have been interesting to find out what happened to James Spencer.

In **November 1916** the following gallantry awards were announced for ex-students of King's School, Canterbury who had enlisted in the army to do their bit for king and country during the First World War.

Acting Paymaster Royal Navy F.T. Spickernell, was **Mentioned in Despatches**.

Lieutenant Colonel E.H.H. Gordon, 9th Battalion, Gordon Highlanders, was awarded the **Distinguished Service Order**.

Captain W.G. Fluke, 2nd Battalion, South Staffordshire Regiment, was awarded the **Distinguished Service Order**.

Commander J.W. Carrington, Royal Navy, was awarded the **Distinguished Service Order**.

Lieutenant H.W.S. Husbands, Royal Engineers, was awarded the **Distinguished Service Order**.

Second Lieutenant F.M. Deighton, Royal Field Artillery, was awarded the **Military Cross**.

Major D.K. Anderson, The Buffs (East Kent Regiment) was awarded the **Military Cross**.

Lieutenant L.C. Watson, New Zealanders, was awarded the **Military Cross**.

Major J.R. Rowan Robinson, Supply and Transport Corps, was awarded the **Distinguished Conduct Medal**.

An example of the bloody excesses of 1916 can quite clearly be found in the Battle of the Somme, which finally ended on 18 November, and has since gone down in history as one of the bloodiest that Britain has ever been involved in. It is estimated that some 400,000 British troops were killed during the four and a half months of fighting, with tens of thousands more who were wounded. More than 19,000 were killed on the first day alone, figures that Field Marshal Sir Douglas Haig was said to have referred to the following morning as not being too bad in the circumstances. The result, 6 miles of enemy territory gained along a 16-mile front. The need for the battle is questionable when looked at purely from a British perspective. It was fought not out of necessity, but a need to help the beleaguered French at Verdun who had been fighting the Germans there since 21 February 1916. It was hoped that a British attack on the Somme would draw German forces away from Verdun and, in doing so, greatly help the French. By the time the fighting had come to an end at Verdun on 18 December 1918, the French had sustained an estimated 377,231 casualties of whom 162,308 were either killed or missing.

Military Cross.

With this information in mind, the following piece on the topic of recruitment and the need for even more men to enlist in the British Army has, I feel, a bit more relevance.

Saturday, 2 December 1916 saw an official article in relation to military recruitment appear in the *Thanet Advertiser* newspaper.

Distinguished Conduct Medal.

It has been brought to notice that the publication of names in the newspaper, even though nothing was said about their being absentees, tends to cast reflection on individuals. That there was no such intention will be clear from the wording of the notice which is now being here used.

The Headquarters Recruiting Officer, 3rd Regimental District Recruiting Area, Canterbury, asks for information regarding the following men, as to whether they

(a) Have joined the Army;

(a) Are excepted from the provisions of the Military Services Act 1916;

(b) Are in possession of a definite certificate or badge exempting them from liability for Military Service;

(c) Are in a reserved occupation;

(d) Have moved to another district, etc., etc.

Military Services Act Poster.

The above information is required to complete records in Recruiting Offices, and any communication will be treated in strict confidence.

Dampier Palmer, Captain
Head Quarters Recruiting Office, 3rd Recruiting Area.

The list of men the military authorities were looking to locate had more than 220 names on it of men from all over the Kent area, including Dover, Folkestone, Hythe, Sandgate, and the following eight men from Canterbury.

- Cecil H. **Twyman**, 39 Wincheap Street, Canterbury. 23 years of age.
- George **Turner**, 50 St Peter's Place, Canterbury. 33 years of age.
- Winsley **Davey**, 71 St Peter's Place, Canterbury. 39 years of age.
- Albert L. **Duncan**, 12 Northgate Street, Canterbury. 31 years of age.
- Henry J.B. **Jacobs**, 17 Castle Street, Canterbury. 40 years of age.
- Harry **Dean**, 14 Orange Street, Canterbury. 33 years of age.
- William G. **Ralfe**, 4 Burgate Lane, Canterbury. 32 years of age.
- Robert **Cook**, Agricultural Bailiff, Canterbury.

Sometimes men's names appeared on these lists incorrectly, for a host of different reasons. The first of the Canterbury men on that list is of particular interest, as a check of the Commonwealth War Graves Commission website shows that a 22-year-old Private G/9329 Cecil Herbert **Twyman**, from Canterbury, served with the 6th Battalion, The Buffs (East Kent Regiment) and was killed in action on 14 July 1916. He has no known grave but his name is commemorated on the Thiepval Memorial, which is situated in the Somme region.

If this is the same man, then how he managed to appear on the list more than four months after he had been killed in action serving his country, remains a mystery.

We shall never know what the outcome would have been if there had been a negotiated peace settlement during the course of 1916, but one thing is for certain, in the short term at least, it would have saved the lives of 336,119 British and Empire soldiers, and prevented so much pain and suffering to the loved ones of these brave men.

CHAPTER FOUR

1917 – Seeing it Through

This was the fourth year of the war, much longer than anyone could have possibly anticipated it would have lasted for, and still there was no end in sight. Once again, it was a year that saw numerous different events take place on the world stage which could be said to have had a major effect on the war, which included the sinking of a ship, an abdication and an air attack on London.

Throughout the course of the year, at least seventy-two men who were either from, or who had connections with Canterbury, died as a result of their involvement in the war. This included fourteen men who were serving with The Buffs (East Kent Regiment) and another ten who served with the Queen's Own (Royal West Kent Regiment).

On **Monday, 15 January 1917** a lecture was given by Adjutant Charles Peck at the Salvation Army Hall, in White House Lane, Canterbury, in connection with General Booth's Women's Migration Scheme. It attracted a large audience, which not surprisingly was made up largely of women. The scheme was primarily aimed at women widowed by the war, or single women, and looked to facilitate the migration of such women whose circumstances were likely to be improved by migration to overseas dominions such as Canada, Australia, New Zealand, or South Africa, after the end of the war. Under the scheme, worthy widows living in unsatisfactory environments in Britain were to be given the opportunity of taking advantage of the better conditions available for industrious women in the Overseas Dominions of the Empire.

Widows and any children they had, who became part of the scheme, were under the care of the army for up to four years, or until their circumstances had progressed sufficiently well for the military guardianship to be dispensed with. In the unlikely event of a widow failing to find a suitor during the four year time period she would have to return home to the UK.

This scheme was simply a replication of something similar that the army already had in place, and which had seen several hundred British widows and

Soldiers in the Trenches.

their children happily resettled throughout Canada, Australia, New Zealand and South Africa. It was a well-respected scheme which had a long and successful history attached to it and was known for having the permanent welfare of the women and children concerned at heart, as did the Dominion nations who received these widows and their families. It was hoped that some of the widows and single women from Canterbury would become involved in the scheme to benefit themselves and their families.

Saturday, 20 January 1917 saw one of the very best concerts that had been given by Mr W.J. Moor's Dover Concert Parties; it took place at St George's YMCA Hall in Canterbury. Having been in the city many times before, the entertainers received a by now customary hearty welcome from the crowd who had turned up to see them. The large hall was 'packed to the rafters', standing room only was the order of the day, such was the demand to get in to see what was on offer. Most of the audience appeared to be either soldiers or sailors, with just a few civilians dotted amongst the great throng of wildly enthusiastic individuals.

The quartet of lady vocalists, Miss Vera Pilcher, Mrs W. Lewis, Miss Alma Shipway and Miss Elsie Baker, were all in excellent voice and included many songs from their extensive repertoire. When finished, it was encore after encore before they were eventually allowed to finish their evening's work, and then only after they had each come back on stage individually to be applauded for their efforts.

Next it was the turn of Lance Corporal French of the Royal Engineers to entertain the crowd, a noted comedian who was on top form and kept the audience in fits of laughter throughout his performance. Once again, with his part of the show at an end, it was encore after encore before he was finally allowed to disappear behind the stage curtain for a final time.

Another act that was humour based was that of Private Marsland of the Middlesex Regiment, whose comic songs were much to the liking of the appreciative audience. Yet again it was the demand for encore after encore that was evidence of how good his performance had been.

The Misses Fridays, who skilfully played mandolin duets, were extremely popular, and when they were joined by Miss E. Baker on the piano, and Mr Moor on the 'bones and bells', in a lively and vibrant selection of musical ditties, the exuberant applause was almost deafening. I have to admit that I have absolutely no idea what the equivalent of 'bones and bells' would be today, or if in fact there is still an equivalent in existence. Once again an encore was the order of the day before all four artistes were allowed to leave.

German SM U-50.

It was a memorable evening for all concerned enjoyed by players and audience alike, and was what might be called good old-fashioned value for money. An audience not only suitably entertained, but allowed to forget their personal woes along with the strains and stresses that went with being part of a nation at war, if only for just a few short hours.

In **February 1917,** the tragic news was received of the death of Private G/13020 Richard Thomas Birch of the 7th Battalion, The Buffs (East Kent Regiment) who was 23 years of age and the only son of Thomas and Annie Birch of Marshside, Chislet, near Canterbury, although they had two younger daughters, Elizabeth and Harriet, also living at home with them. Richard initially enlisted in the Royal East Kent Mounted Rifles in May 1915, and was sent out to France in September 1916 where he was killed in action just two months later, on 18 November 1916, which was the final day of the Battle of the Somme. His body was never recovered which is possibly why it took so long to officially confirm his death, but his name is commemorated on the Thiepval Memorial. Prior to enlisting in the army he had been employed for several years by Mr George Spratt of Hawthorne, Chislet, who was a farmer.

Sunday, 25 February 1917 saw the sinking of the Cunard ocean liner RMS *Laconia*, by the German submarine, SM *U-50*, 6 miles north of Fastnet, which is off the southerly most tip of Ireland, whilst returning to England from America. The Laconia had a crew of 217 and was carrying 75 passengers when it was struck by two torpedoes fired by the *U-50*. Six of the crew and six passengers, which included two Americans, were killed in the attack. This is often quoted as one of the reasons behind America's entry into the First World War on the side of the Allies.

On the afternoon of **Friday, 9 March 1917,** a meeting took place that was presided over by the mayor, and held in his office at the Guildhall, Canterbury. The purpose of the meeting was to hear from Major Herbert who was present in his capacity as the representative of the Director General of National Service, and for him to provide an in-depth description of what the scheme was all about. The main message which came across appeared to be that 'an active canvassing campaign for volunteers should be instituted in which the services of the local political associations should be obtained' and 'that the assistance of the political agents of all parties should be obtained as they are fully experienced in the kind of work required, and have previously rendered invaluable service during the military recruiting campaigns.' Major Herbert also made the suggestion that the services of teachers should be sought in the matter of clerical assistance, as their natural ability in such areas would prove extremely useful and, as on previous occasions of such need, they were found to be most ready, willing and able to assist.

This was yet another example of how much volunteer work was undertaken on the home front by willing individuals who, because of many different reasons, were unable to pick up a rifle and stand their watch, but who still wanted to do their bit as best they could for the greater good of the nation.

Thursday, 15 March 1917 saw the abdication of the Russian, Tsar Nicholas ll.

America declared war on Germany on **6 April 1917**, but no sooner had she done so than French troops displayed the first signs of unrest and displeasure towards their senior officers, when they gave serious consideration to mutinying at Aisne.

News was received in **April 1917** of the death of Second Lieutenant Henry Gordon Wright, who was 32 years of age and a married man, who was serving with the 5th Battalion and attached to the 11th Battalion, Middlesex Regiment in France. His parents, Joseph and Fanny Wright, of 12 London Road, Canterbury, were informed of their son's death in a letter from his commanding officer. They read how he was killed in action on Monday, 9 April 1917 whilst leading his men in an attack on enemy held trenches. He is buried at the Sainte Catherine British Cemetery in the Pas de Calais region of France.

In his younger years, Second Lieutenant Wright had for several years been a chorister at Canterbury Cathedral where, as he himself progressed, he also began helping to teach and train new members who were starting out as choristers. After attending St Mark's training college in Chelsea, he was in 1909 appointed to the position of Art Master at the Herbert Strutt Grammar School and Pupil Teacher Centre at Belper in Derbyshire, a position which he held up until the time of receiving his commission in the army.

In **May 1917,** following a meeting of the Dover Vigilance Committee, in the Council Chamber, an address was given later that day at a public meeting by Mrs Spooner, the wife of Archdeacon Spooner of Maidstone. The chairman of the committee first informed the meeting that the question of Women Patrols had been discussed some eighteen months previously, but at that time it was not felt practicable, though many at the meeting believed it would be of value. Mrs Spooner went on to describe the work of Women Patrols at Canterbury where they were believed to be of very great value. The chief constable at Canterbury had met with Mrs Spooner before their work in the city had first begun, and told her that Women Patrols were very much wanted. The patrol work was not police work though, he said, it would be fair to describe it as 'friendly police work'. One of the rules observed by the patrols was not to speak to a female if she was speaking with a soldier, unless they genuinely felt that the woman in question was 'in some difficulty', polite speak for saying that she had bitten off a bit more than she could chew. She was out of her depth, or put simply she was struggling to cope with the situation she found herself in. But, Mrs Spooner said, she could assure everybody that the very presence of the patrols raised the standard of the behaviour of the girls and women who were in the area at the time.

Female Police Officer.

The patrols were asked by the police to help in cases involving women and this was a great step forward, for they felt it was extremely useful to have the ladies of the Women's Patrols deal with women who came to the attention of the police for whatever reason. With regard to the patrol work that had been carried out at Canterbury, they had received unexpected appreciation from the army, the clergy, and even more surprisingly, the police. Mrs Spooner explained that to form their patrol at Canterbury, they had called a meeting and asked various members of the clergy to invite suitable members of their congregations to assist in the work. The person in charge of the patrols and the women who were part of them was a Mrs Prentice, the wife of Doctor Prentice of Canterbury. To any town wanting to form a patrol, a lady organiser would be sent from the London headquarters, initially for a two-week period, totally free of charge if accommodation were provided, and longer by way of an agreed arrangement.

In the Canterbury patrol there were eight women who went out in pairs, and at no time and in no circumstances would a woman be allowed to patrol on her own.

In thanking Mrs Spooner for providing her lecture, the chairman referred to the potential danger which girls and women placed themselves in by being out and around the town of Dover late in to the evenings, he hoped that Dover would follow in the footsteps of Canterbury and introduce Women Patrols.

Sunday, 17 June 1917 saw a massive German air raid on London, by Gotha bomber aircraft. It was a notable event which resulted in the deaths of 158 civilians and a further 425 who were wounded, the worst British civilian casualties of the entire war.

On **Friday, 22 June 1917** an accident occurred during 'bombing practice' or what today would be called grenade throwing, at Canterbury, and sadly resulted in the death of 27-year-old Corporal 241287 Bert Oswald Hilton, a married man who lived with his wife, Beatrice, at 22 London Road, Staines, Middlesex. He was serving with the 2nd/8th Battalion, Middlesex Regiment, and was stationed in the city.

The circumstances of the soldier's death were investigated by the Coroner, Mr John Plummer, at an inquest which took place at the Canterbury Military Hospital the following day. It was established that prior to having enlisted in the army, Corporal Hilton had worked as a barman at the Crown and Anchor Inn, at Staines.

Lieutenant John Eric S. Goss was the bombing officer of the 2nd/8th Battalion, Middlesex Regiment, and was stationed at Scotland Hills, Canterbury. He gave evidence to the inquest that on Wednesday, 6 June 1917, he was in charge of a group of men who were undertaking grenade throwing training, and that Corporal Hilton was the sixth man of the group to throw. At the time he was wearing his steel helmet and gas mask, and was handed a live grenade whilst standing in the area of what was designated as the throwing area. Lieutenant Goss saw Corporal Hilton remove the pin from the

Grenade throwing.

grenade, but as he leant back slightly and began to swing his right arm over his head, his helmet fell off and caught his right arm in its fall. He then saw the grenade leave the corporal's hand but then lost sight of its trajectory. The bombing sergeant who was standing behind the corporal in the bombing bay, shouted out a warning followed by a similar warning from Lieutenant Goss who called out to him to follow him as he made his way around the corner and out of the bombing bay, but for some reason Corporal Hilton failed to follow him. Lieutenant Goss then heard an explosion followed by a cry. He ran back towards the bombing bay, and as he did so he saw Corporal Hilton running towards him. He immediately had his wounds tended to and was taken to the nearby military hospital.

In further evidence, Lieutenant Goss explained how there was a chance of a soldier's helmet falling off whilst in the process of throwing a grenade, but it should not do so if it was secured as it should be by the chin strap being tightened. He did not know why Corporal Hilton hadn't following him out of the bombing bay faster than he did, but he agreed with the coroner's suggestion that it was possible that Corporal Hilton had instinctively stopped to pick up his helmet.

Sergeant John Davis Monick corroborated the evidence provided by Lieutenant Goss. He then further explained to the inquest that once a pin is removed from a grenade, there was only five seconds before it would explode. He saw Corporal Hilton's helmet fall off his head and inadvertently knock the grenade out of his hand, so he immediately blew his whistle as a warning to all to seek shelter, and shouted out to both the lieutenant and Corporal Hilton to run for cover. He saw them both start to run from the bay and the next thing he knew was that the grenade had exploded and he saw Corporal Hilton come staggering round the traverse of the bay. Along with Lieutenant Goss, he administered first aid to the wounded man, after which time he was removed to the military hospital.

Doctor Charles E. Murphy of the Royal Army Medical Corps, told the inquest that he treated Corporal Hilton at the Canterbury Military Hospital on Wednesday, 6 June 1917. His wounds were severe and consisted of injuries to his right arm, right thigh and leg. On Friday, 8 June gangrene had developed in the man's right leg necessitating its amputation. He survived the shock of having to have his leg amputated only to subsequently have gangrene develop in his left breast and he died from exhaustion due to blood poisoning.

Once the coroner had heard all of the available evidence, he provided the jury with a summation of it, who then returned a verdict of 'Accidental Death'.

Corporal Hilton, who was a popular and well-liked figure amongst both the officers and men of his battalion, was buried with full military honours at the Canterbury Cemetery on Monday, 11 June 1917.

July 1917 saw the Duke of Argyll protest, in the strongest possible terms, in relation to comments which had been made by the Archbishop of Canterbury in relation to 'reprisals' against Germany for the raids her pilots and airmen had carried out over English towns and cities, which killed many British civilians in the process.

The duke commented on how the archbishop spoke of the 'quibbling consciences of the Episcopate' and observed that 'Prelates selected for their proficiency in dead languages' and to whom science appeared to be a bewildering subject and highly 'apocalyptic', have the utmost difficulty in realising the enormous progress which aviation had reached, along with the increasing dangers which the civil population would have to endure before the war was at an end. The duke felt that the archbishop and other, what he referred to as 'confused thinkers' were too cautious to have openly defined what they considered to be military objectives. He assured the archbishop and his followers that there would be few towns and villages throughout the nation that would escape death and large-scale destruction from German air attacks the longer the war continued, and they as Britain's enemy would not lose a second's sleep over the outcomes of their actions. They had absolutely no qualms whatsoever, the duke said, in attacking munitions factories which they

Archbishop of Canterbury.

saw as legitimate military targets which, it could be argued, they might well be. The Germans clearly knew that the vast majority of people who worked in these factories were women and girls, but did that stop the Germans from targeting them, did they think about the women and girls that they would kill by their actions? No. Not for one second. It was exactly the same with any factory that was being used to make anything for the army, down to boots and bandages.

Although mindful of his words, the duke, no doubt because he did not want to be seen to be attacking the church which after all played such an important part in people's everyday lives, spoke eloquently when broadly referring to the Archbishop of Canterbury and his colleagues, and their particular take on the war as being 'muddle-headed thinking'. The war was not going to be won by going back to using coracles and bows and arrows, and the general scrapping of their modern equivalents, but by using every conceivable method and device that military science had put into the hands of nations in order to defend themselves.

The futile discussions about a doctrine of intention, the duke said, were largely due to the use of the word 'reprisals'. After all, what is war? If the words 'counter-raid' helped 'pour balm on the bishop's opinions, then pray let us use them. 'Disease,' he said, 'often demanded strange sedatives.'

Tuesday, 31 July 1917 saw the start of the Battle of Passchendaele, also known as the Third Battle of Ypres, which continued until 10 November 1917. Over the years there have been variations of the number of casualties on both sides, some of which came down to what each side classified as being a casualty, and also down to which parts of the overall fighting were included, such as the Battle of Cambrai. A fair estimate, according to Richard Holmes, a former British soldier and military historian, was that both sides suffered somewhere in the region of 260,000 casualties, although these figures have also been estimated to have been much higher.

Friday, 3 August 1917 saw 38-year-old Sergeant Charles William Jones of the Dragoon Guards, before the Canterbury Police Court. He was charged with bigamy, or as it was referred to at the time, 'feloniously marrying'. The unfortunate lady who he married, whilst still married to his first wife, Nellie Maria Jones, was Minnie Blake of Canterbury.

Mr W. Ley, who appeared for the Director of Public Prosecutions, outlined the facts of the case. In 1905 Sergeant Jones married a woman, also by the name of Blake, and they lived in Caterham, Surrey. They were happily married, and their seven children were born between 1905 and 1914.

At the outbreak of the war Jones was a reservist in the army, whilst working as an attendant at an undisclosed asylum which came under the auspices of the Metropolitan Asylums Board. He enlisted in the 3rd Dragoon Guards, which meant he was away from home undergoing his military training, but he wrote to his wife regularly and visited her whenever he could. It would appear, however, that no sooner had he arrived in Canterbury, where he was barracked, than he met and got to know a local lady by the name of Miss Minnie Blake. In no time at all they were an item, or as it was called in those days, 'walking out together'. Miss Blake asked Jones on more than one occasion if he was married, to which he replied that he wasn't, even replying on one occasion that they wouldn't be 'walking out together' if he were married to another. They subsequently became engaged and Jones asked Miss Blake if she would marry him after the war. On the strength of a promise of marriage and commitment, Miss Blake was happy for intimacy to take place between them. So keen was Jones for them to marry, that they didn't wait until the war's end, instead they married on 23 November 1916 in Canterbury. As they were married she understandably asked him for money but he never provided any, claiming that he could not provide her with a military separation allowance as was building an allotment for his mother, who was looking after his invalid father. The real reason why he couldn't make any such payment to Minnie was because it was already being paid to his wife and their seven children.

With the war continuing, Jones was sent out to France, and whilst there he wrote to Minnie on several occasions, but never sent her any money. In the course of time Jones's secret came out after the two Mrs Jones's met up, how that came about exactly is unclear, but meet they did. When confronted with the situation in France by his senior officers, he replied, 'I was almost continually under the influence of drink during the time I was walking out with Minnie Blake. It is possible I might have married her, but I do not remember doing so.' The Bench heard a somewhat different account which suggested that he was perfectly sober whilst walking out with Minnie and when he married her.

After being confronted in France with what he had done, he eventually admitted his wrong doing and said that he was going to give himself up when he returned to England.

Nellie Maria Jones confirmed to the court that her marriage with Jones had been a perfectly happy one, and she still had feelings for him. Minnie Blake's feelings towards him were not recorded. Jones was committed for trial at the next county Assizes and was released on bail.

An article appeared in the *Bedfordshire Times and Independent* newspaper, dated **Friday, 14 September 1917** announcing the death of 36-year-old Second Lieutenant Charles Edmund Kirk, who had been serving with the 6th Battalion, Bedfordshire Regiment. He was the second son of Mrs Kirk, who lived at 22 Ampthill Street, Bedford, a widow who had lost two other sons in the war. Charles (4421) had enlisted in the 7th Dragoon Guards, also known as the Black Horse, when he was just 18 years of age, at Bedford, on 20 June 1898. He reached the rank of Squadron Sergeant Major, in 1908 left Canterbury, and for the next two years he was stationed in Egypt, before then being transferred to Secunderabad in India, where he remained until the outbreak of the First World War. From there he was sent to France where he saw quite a bit of active service.

In May 1917 he was gazetted, in the field as a Second Lieutenant, by none other than General Sir Douglas Haig, and was posted to the Bedfordshire Regiment before returning to France with them just two months later in July. Within a month he was dead, killed in action on Sunday, 5 August 1917, although it then took a further five weeks for that information to be received back home in England.

His wife, Hilda May Kirk, and their two young sons, who lived at 3 Cossington Road, Canterbury, received a letter from Charles's commanding officer. The eldest of the two sons, Charles Cyril Kirk, was born on 22 December 1908, at the Citadel Hospital in Cairo, Egypt. Herbert Arthur Kirk was born in Secunderabad, India.

> We were proud to have your husband as an officer, and although he had not been with us long, he became very popular with his brother officers, and the men of his platoon were devoted to him. One feels that we have not only lost a real good officer, but a brave one.

Lieutenant Kirk was an experienced soldier who served through the Second Boer War between 1899 and 1902, during which time he was mentioned in despatches for meritorious conduct. He had also been awarded the General Service Medal for 18 years' service. Charles's nearly 19 years' service was spent as follows.

Home: 20 June 1898 – 7 February 1900

South Africa: 8 February 1900 – 27 June 1903

Home: 28 June 1903 – 22 September 1908

Egypt: 23 September 1908 – 2 October 1910

India: 3 October 1910 – 20 September 1914

Home Voyage: 21 September 1914 – 12 October 1914

France: 13 October 1914 – 19 November 1915

Home: 20 November 1915 – 21 December 1916

France: 22 December 1916 – 12 June 1917.

The last entry outlining Charles military service is slightly at odds, as he was killed in action in France on 5 August 1917.

In a letter, which is dated 26 November 1917 and attached to Charles Kirk's army service record, Hilda wrote to the Secretary of the War Office requesting birth certificates for both of her sons. At the time, she was living at 18 Havelock Street, Canterbury. Somewhat intriguingly, she says in the letter that she requires the birth certificates, 'for Masonic purposes by December 5th.'

Sunday, 14 October 1917 saw the death of Lieutenant John Vernon Campbell-Orde, but he wasn't killed by a bullet or a bomb on the battlefields of France, instead he met his end in a car crash on the Dover Road, near Canterbury.

An inquest took place on Monday, 15 October at No. 1 Military Hospital, Canterbury. It appears that he survived the initial crash but died subsequent to it. An initially unnamed witness said that Campbell-Orde was refused admission to the Kent and Canterbury Hospital, which resulted in the authorities having to telephone the military hospital, where the staff were prepared to admit him. But when the hospital was later contacted by elements of the Press, they refuted this allegation and said that when Campbell-Orde was brought to the hospital by friends, they were informed that there were no private wards available but that he could be admitted on to one of the hospital's general wards. It was the friends' insistence on having a private ward which resulted in the delay in him receiving medical treatment. The matron of the Kent and Canterbury Hospital then had to phone the military hospital to establish if they had a private ward available, which they did, so Campbell-Orde's friends then decided to drive him there. Whether the delay in him receiving medical treatment had anything to do with his death, is unclear.

Campbell-Orde was the son of Sir Arthur and Lady Campbell-Orde of Kilmory, Lochgilphead, Argyll.

On Saturday, 17 November 1917 it was reported in the *Whitstable Times* and *Herne Bay Herald,* that Second Lieutenant R.J. Stockdale, of the Durham Light Infantry, had been wounded. His parents, Mr and Mrs R. Stockdale, lived at Hanover Lodge, Canterbury.

Two Canterbury men were awarded the Military Medal, for acts of bravery. Private G/12980 William **Arman**, who served with the East Kent Regiment and prior to joining the army, lived at 3 St Jacobs Place, Wincheap, Canterbury.

He had enlisted at Canterbury on 3 May 1915. During his time with the regiment, he served with the 3rd/1st, 2nd/1st, 4th, 7th, 3rd, Depot, and 1st battalions, East Kent Regiment. For a period of three days between 25 and 28 July 1918, he also served with the 38th Company Labour Corps, before being posted back to 1st Battalion, The Buffs.

His army service record shows that he first arrived in France on 22 September 1916 at No. 38 Infantry Base, Etaples. It also includes an entry about the award of his Military Medal which it also shows was included in the *London Gazette* on 2 November 1917. This was immediately followed by an entry showing that he had been granted a period of fourteen days leave to the UK, one would imagine, in connection to the award of his Military Medal which meant that he would have been due back with his unit on 16 November. The next entry on his army service record is dated 22 November and shows that he had forfeited one day's pay for 'absence', suggesting that he had arrived back from his leave one day late, maybe due to having over celebrated the award of his Military Medal.

William spent three months in the 3rd Western General Hospital in Cardiff, as a result of having sustained a gunshot wound to the area of his left elbow, which was described as been superficial with no evidence of any fracture.

Royal Flying Corps.

He survived the war and was eventually demobilised on 13 March 1919.

The other man was Private G/2868 Richard G. **Hobbs**, who served with the 8th Battalion, Queens (Royal West Surrey Regiment).

Trumpet Major F. **Sladden**, Royal East Kent Yeomanry, who left England in 1915 and served with both the Mediterranean and the Egyptian Expeditionary Forces, had in recent times been transferred to the Camel Corps and then became attached to an overseas section of the Royal Flying Corps. This was the second son that Walter and Rosa Sladden had serving with the Royal Flying Corps; First Class Air Mechanic, Stan Sladden, had served with them since the early months of the war. The Sladden family lived at 122 Wincheap Street, Canterbury.

Private G/18679 Robert Samuel **Escott** was serving with The Buffs (East Kent Regiment) when he was killed in action on the Western Front on Friday, 12 October 1917, with confirmation of his death only reaching his wife, Florence, who he married in 1912, and his parents, Robert and Edith Escott, about a month later. Prior to the war his home was in Canterbury, and for some thirteen years he had worked in an office in the city's Burgate Street. The 1911 census showed him living with his parents at 20 Lower Bridge Street, Canterbury, along with his four sisters, Edith, Constance, Florence and Doris.

He enlisted in the army in the early part of 1916 and was sent out to France in November of that year. He was a married man and left behind a

Tyne Cot Memorial.

widow and two young children. His parents also lived in Canterbury, at Lower Bridge Street.

He has no known grave but his name is commemorated on the Tyne Cot Memorial, which is situated in the West-Vlaanderen region of Belgium. His brother, Frederick, was already serving in the military before the outbreak of the war. The 1911 census records that he was with the 21st Lancers, stationed in Egypt. His army service record has not survived, but he did survive the war.

Tuesday, 20 November 1917 saw the beginning of the Battle of Cambrai, which continued on until 7 December 1917. It was remembered more for the fact that it saw the single largest number of tanks used by the British in any battle, throughout the entire war.

On **Saturday, 8 December 1917** two tablets were unveiled in the stately nave at Canterbury Cathedral to commemorate the gallant part that HMS *Kent* played in the decisive victory in the sea battle which took place off the Falkland Islands.

Present at the ceremony were, amongst others, Captain Allen, CB, Royal Navy, Commander Bedford, Commander Wharten, Commander Andrew, Lieutenant Commander Harvey, and Surgeon R. Burn, all officers of HMS Kent. Senior military officers were also in attendance. The honour of unveiling

HMS Kent.

the tablet went to Lady Northbourne. A separate marble memorial which was paid for by the officers and crew of HMS *Kent* to commemorate their comrades who were killed during the battle, was unveiled by Captain Allen.

The Dean of Canterbury in an address, remarked that the great naval victory of the Falklands had been described as the most decisive action of the present war. By that victory he said, 'the flag of Germany, had been swept from the seas' making life for vessels of the British Royal Navy and her Allies, that much safer. With one of the ships that played a significant part in that victory bearing the county name of Kent, it was a proud moment for everybody connected with the county.

The Battle of the Falkland Islands took place on 8 December 1914, in the South Atlantic and resulted in the total destruction of Germany's East Asia Squadron. By the time the battle was over, the British had not lost a single vessel. Their casualties were ten men killed with a further nineteen wounded. The German losses were, two armoured cruisers sunk, two light cruisers sunk, with two transport vessels captured. Their casualties were 1,871 men killed, and 215 men captured.

HMS Torrent.

From what I can tell, the last man from Canterbury to fall in the war during the course of 1917, was 22-year-old Lieutenant Alec Norman **Kennedy** of the Royal Navy, who died on 23 December 1917. He was a crew member of HMS *Torrent*, a Royal Navy R-class destroyer, which had only been launched on 26 November 1916, and became part of the 10th Destroyer Flotilla of the Harwich Force. Part of their duties consisted of undertaking convoys to and from Holland. On 22 December 1917, *Torrent* was part of a convoy taking a number of vessels to the Hook of Holland. It was a successful journey, although one of the escort vessels, the destroyer HMS *Valkyrie* struck a mine and was badly damaged, so much so that she had to be towed back to Harwich by one of the other escort vessels. The remainder of the escort which included the *Torrent*, after having reached the Hook, waited near the Maas Light Bouy for the returning convoy.

At about 2 am on 23 December 1917, HMS *Torrent*, *Surprise*, *Tornado* and *Radiant* suddenly found themselves in a German minefield. Before any of the Royal Navy vessels realised what was happening, *Torrent* had struck one of the mines. *Surprise* and *Tornado* immediately went to *Torrent's* assistance in an effort to aid her crew, but before they got close enough to do so, *Torrent* struck yet another mine and sank soon afterwards. Undeterred by the obvious dangers that they now found themselves in, *Surprise* and *Tornado* then attempted to rescue survivors from the sea but, sadly, it wasn't long before both vessels also struck mines and suffered the same fate as *Torrent*. The only ship left afloat and undamaged was *Radiant,* who now had the task of trying to save as many crew members from each of the ships as she could. The total number of officers and men who perished on the lost ships was 252. Out of *Torrent's* crew of 71 officers and men, 68 of them including Alec, were killed.

The 1911 census showed Alec's parents, Albert and Ada Kennedy, living at 'Fairlawn', Whitstable Road, Canterbury, with their younger son Reginald, who was 10 years old, and their daughter Irene, who was 8.

CHAPTER FIVE

1918 – The Final Push

Although people didn't know it at the time, as 1917 came to an end and 1918 began in earnest, it was to be the final year of the war, but it would come at a very high cost. According to the Commonwealth War Graves Commission, here are the losses sustained by Britain and the other Empire nations from 1 January 1918 up to and including 11 November 1918:

Australia	14,275
Britain	209,686
Canada	17,883
India	13,648
New Zealand	4,899
South Africa	3,011

That is a total of 263,402 men who were killed, and when divided by the number of days the war went on for during that final year, it equates to 836 men killed every day. Of the men killed during that final eleven months of the war, forty-three of them were from Canterbury or had Canterbury connections.

Wednesday, 30 January 1918 saw the death of 22-year-old Able Seaman J/15734 Andrew Bert **Wilson** of the Royal Navy, whilst serving as the crew of HMS *Wellholme*. He was killed in action when the *Wellholme* was attacked by a German submarine in the English Channel. His body was never recovered, he has no known grave, but his name is commemorated on the Portsmouth Naval Memorial.

His parents, William and Dorothy Wilson, lived at 54 Dover Street, Canterbury.

Thursday, 21 March 1918 saw the death of 31-year-old Sergeant SE/5304 Stanley Herbert **Cavell**, whilst serving with the Army Veterinary Corps, but who was attached to the 177th Brigade, Royal Field Artillery, when he was killed in action. He has no known grave, but his name is commemorated on the Ploegsteert Memorial in Hainaut, Belgium.

After the war, Stanley's widow, who by then had remarried and become Mrs Louise Yarsley Barnett, was living at 2 Alicia Vilas, Chatham, Canterbury.

Friday, 22 March 1918 saw the death of 28-year-old Stoker 1st Class K/530 Sidney George **Mount**, crew member of HMS *Gaillardia* and who was killed in action. He has no known grave, but his name is commemorated on the Chatham Naval Memorial. He had enlisted in the Royal Navy on 8 January 1911.

HMS *Gaillardia* was an Aubretia-class sloop of the British Royal Navy and under the command of Commander John Sharpey Schafer, when she was sunk after having struck a mine, believed to have been a British one, in the North Sea.

A soldier of the Great War.

Sidney's mother, Mrs Ann Jane Deverson, lived at 1 Rose Cottage, Westmarsh, Ash, near Canterbury. Sidney was just 1-year-old when his father George William Mount died in 1892 when he was 27 years of age. Ann, his mother, married William Edmund Deverson, in August 1893, when Sidney was just 2.

The same date also saw the death of 35-year-old Able Seaman 206679 Percy John **Pout**, another crew member of HMS *Gaillardia* killed in action. He has no known grave, but his name is commemorated on the Chatham Naval Memorial.

His parents, Frederick and Lucy Pout, lived at 'Broadoak', Sturry, Canterbury.

Friday, 22 March 1918 saw the death of Corporal G/8135 W **Drury**, who was serving with the 1st Battalion, The Buffs, (East Kent Regiment). He is buried at the St Pierre Cemetery at Amiens, which is situated in the Somme region.

His father, Mr G. Drury, lived at 84 Black Griffin Lane, Canterbury.

Sunday, 24 March 1918 saw the death of 30-year-old Sergeant 7759 Frederick Walter **Sheaff**, who was serving with the 3rd (King's Own) Hussars, when he was killed in action. He has no known grave, but his name is commemorated on the Pozieres Memorial, which is situated in the Somme region.

HMS Gaillardia.

His mother, Mrs Sarah Sheaff, lived at The Square, Chilham, Canterbury.

Monday, 25 March 1918 saw the death of 25-year-old Gunner 157151 A.T.W. **Addy**, who at the time was serving with the 299th Siege Battery, Royal Garrison Artillery, when he died of his wounds and was buried at the St Pierre Cemetery, Amiens, in the Somme region.

His parents, Alfred and Agnes Addy, lived at Sterling Lodge, Petham, Canterbury.

Tuesday, 26 March 1918 saw the death of 22-year-old Rifleman 593480 Alfred **Beaumont**, who was serving with the 1st/18th (London Irish Rifles) Battalion, London Regiment, when he was killed in action. He has no known grave, but his name is commemorated on the Arras Memorial, which is located in the Pas de Calais region of France.

His parents, Frederick and Kezia Beaumont, lived at 14 Cross Street, St Dunstan's, Canterbury.

Wednesday, 3 April 1918 saw the death of 38-year-old Private 3252 Frank **Amiel** of the 35th Battalion, Australian Infantry, Australian Imperial Force, who was killed in action and buried at the Adelaide Cemetery at Villers-Bretonneux, which is situated in the Somme region.

Pozieres Memorial.

Frank was born in Deal, Kent, whilst his parents lived at 17 Orange Street, Canterbury.

Thursday, 4 April 1918 saw the death of 28-year-old Private 193433 Arthur Frederick **Styles** of the 42nd Battalion, Canadian Infantry (Quebec Regiment), who was killed in action and buried at the Houchin British Cemetery, which is situated in the Pas de Calais region of France.

His parents lived at 61 Sturry Road, Canterbury.

Wednesday, 10 April 1918 saw the death of 25-year-old Albert Frank **Andrews**, a Wireman 2nd Class, Royal Navy and a crew member of HMS *Magic*, an M-class destroyer, when it struck a mine off the coast of Ireland. The ship wasn't sunk but a number of the crew, including Albert, were killed in the subsequent explosion. He has no known grave, but his name is commemorated on the Portsmouth Naval Memorial.

Albert was born in Canterbury.

Thursday, 11 April 1918 saw the death of 17-year-old Private 419142 Cecil F. **Simpson** who served with the 42nd Battalion, Canadian Infantry (Quebec Regiment) when he was killed in action. He is buried at La Chaudiere Military Cemetery, at Vimy, Pas de Calais, France.

He was the foster son of Laura Fruin of 32 Guildford Road, Canterbury.

Sunday, 14 April 1918 saw the death of 25-year-old Private 8074 Patrick Thomas **Kelly**, when he was serving with 'A' Squadron, 19th (Queen Alexandra's Own Royal) Hussars. He died of his wounds and is buried at the Grand-Seraucourt British Cemetery, in the Aisne region of France.

His mother, Emily Kelly, lived at 4 Notley Street, Canterbury.

Monday, 15 April 1918 saw the death of 20-year-old Private 75916 E **Potter** of the 2nd Battalion London Regiment (Royal Fusiliers). He was killed in action and is buried at the Moreuil Communal Cemetery Allied Extension, in the Somme region.

His parents, Frederick and Alice Potter, lived at Longneck House, Waltham, Canterbury.

Wednesday, 17 April 1918 saw the death of 19-year-old Private 42666 Frederick Sidney **Lemar**, who was serving with the 10th Battalion, Lincolnshire Regiment, when he was killed in action. He has no known grave, but his name is commemorated on the Tyne Cot Memorial, which is situated in the West Vlaanderen region of Belgium.

His parents, Benjamin and Emily Lemar, lived at 33 Longport Street, Canterbury.

Friday, 26 April 1918 saw the death of 20-year-old Rifleman 392542 George Thomas **Freeman** of the 9th (Queen Victoria's Rifles) Battalion, London Regiment, attached to the 12th (The Rangers) Battalion, London Regiment. He died of his wounds, which he sustained as the result of a gas attack and is buried at the Etaples Military Cemetery, which is situated in the Pas de Calais region of France.

His parents, Francis and Mary Freeman, lived at 38 Sturry Road, Canterbury.

Friday, 26 April 1918 saw the death of 21-year-old Lieutenant Wolseley Haig **Furley**, of the 3rd Battalion, Scots Guards. He had been mentioned in despatches, and had previously been wounded on 3rd May at the Battle of Monchy-le-Preux, while attached to the regiment's 2nd Battalion. He has no known grave, but his name is commemorated on the Tyne Cot Memorial.

His parents, Frederick and Helen Furley, lived at Sunbury, Canterbury.

Friday, 10 May 1918 saw the death of 19-year-old Private G/25264 Horace Edwin **Deal** of the 1st Battalion, The Buffs (East Kent Regiment). He died of his wounds and is buried at the Esquelbecq Military Cemetery, in the Nord region of France.

His parents, Frederick and Jane Deal, lived at Hill House Farm, Wootton, Canterbury.

Wednesday, 22 May 1918 saw the death of 19-year-old Private 87324 Alfred Lawrence **Hoare** of the 23rd Battalion, Middlesex Regiment. He died of his wounds and is buried at the Boulogne Eastern Cemetery, in the Pas de Calais region of France.

His parents, William and Maria Hoare, lived at Ivy House, Stelling Minnis, Canterbury.

Sunday, 30 June 1918 saw the death of 21-year-old Private 205088 Horace **Sayer** of the 6th Battalion, Queen's Own (Royal West Kent Regiment) when he was killed in action. He has no known grave, but his name is commemorated on the Pozieres Memorial, in the Somme region.

His parents, George and Violet Sayer, lived at Pilot's Cottage, Lower Hardres, Canterbury.

Wednesday, 3 July 1918 saw the death of 20-year-old Private 21180 George Thomas **Marsh**, whilst serving with the 7th Battalion, The Queen's (Royal West Surrey Regiment). He died whilst being held as a prisoner of war at the Niederzwehren Prisoner of War Camp, at Hessen, Germany. Further information about this camp has been included elsewhere in this chapter.

His parents, James and Clara Marsh, lived at 'White House', Ware, Ash, Canterbury.

Saturday, 10 August 1918 saw the death of 25-year-old Corporal 201920 Walter Albert **Harlow** of the 6th Battalion, The Buffs (East Kent Regiment), who was killed in action and buried at the Pernois British Cemetery, Halloy-les-Pernois, which is situated in the Somme region.

His mother, Susannah Harlow, lived at Ivy Cottage, Chilham Lees, near Canterbury.

Saturday, 10 August 1918 saw the death of 27-year-old Private 305978 B.J. **Wilkinson**, whilst serving with the 2nd Battalion, Tank Corps. He is buried at the Bouchoir New British Cemetery, which is situated in the Somme region.

His widow, Alice Keziah Wilkinson, lived at 42 Military Road, Canterbury.

Monday, 19 August 1918 saw the death of 19-year-old Private 535512 Norman Falkner **Fenwick**, who was serving with the 1st/15th (Prince of Wales' Own Civil Service Rifles) Battalion, London Regiment, when he was killed in action, and buried at the Bonnay Communal Cemetery Extension, which is situated in the Somme region.

His connection with the city was that he was educated at Kent College, Canterbury.

Thursday, 22 August 1918 saw the death of 19-year-old Private 26577 Herbert George **Law**, of the 1st/23rd Battalion, London Regiment, who was killed in action and buried at the Bray Vale British Cemetery, which is situated at Bray-sur-Somme, in France. He had previously served with the East Surrey Regiment.

Prior to enlisting in the army he had lived with his parents, Edwin and Minnie Law, at The Bakery, Upstreet, Canterbury. He had an elder brother, Harry, who died in late 1914 soon after the beginning of the First World War, when he was only 16 years of age. There is no suggestion that Harry's death was in any way connected to the war.

Friday, 30 August 1918 saw the death of 28-year-old Sergeant 593390 Ernest George **Ashman** whilst serving with the 1st/18th (London Irish Rifles) London Regiment. He has no known grave, but his name is commemorated on the Vis-en-Artois Memorial, which is situated in the Pas-de-Calais region of France.

He was a married man whose widow, Elizabeth Ashman, lived at 26 Cross Street, St Dunstan's, Canterbury.

Saturday, 31 August 1918 saw the death of 31-year-old Lieutenant Alfred Homewood **Hedgecock** who served with the 57th Battalion, Australian Infantry, Australian Imperial Force. He is buried at the Herbecourt British Cemetery, which is located on the Somme, France.

His parents, Edward and Sarah Hedgecock, lived at 8 Park Street, Deal, Kent, and Alfred was born at Canterbury, Kent

Monday, 2 September 1918 saw the death of 32-year-old Private M/351087 Harry **Wyatt**, serving with the 364th Company, Base Mechanical Transport Depot, Army Service Corps, when he died of his wounds. He is buried at Les Baraques Military Cemetery, at Sangatte, France.

His widow Gertrude Eliza Wyatt, lived at Mystole, Chatham, Canterbury.

Tuesday, 3 September 1918 saw the death of 35-year-old Private 38357 A.W. **Johnson**, whilst serving with the 1st Battalion, Norfolk Regiment. He was killed in action and is buried at the Bagneux British Cemetery, Gezaincourt, France.

His widow, Mrs A.M. Johnson, lived at 28 Alma Street, Canterbury.

Friday, 6 September 1918 saw the death of 28-year-old Rifleman S/12016 Alfred Walter **Vize** who was serving with the 2nd Battalion, Rifle Brigade. He is buried in the Niederzwehren Cemetery at Kassel, which would suggest that when he died of dysentery, he was being held as a prisoner of war at the town's camp, which began taking British and French prisoners in December 1914. A fuller description of the camp can be found with the entry below for George Horace Terry, who died at the same camp and is buried in the same cemetery.

His mother, Rose Matilda Vize, lived in Preston Street, Preston, Canterbury.

Monday, 9 September 1918 saw the death of 26-year-old Lance Corporal 505135 Maurice Charles **Rickarby**, of the 2nd Battalion, Kings Royal Rifle Corps. He died of the wounds he sustained as the result of a gas attack, and is another of those buried at the Terlincthun British Cemetery, Wimille.

His parents, Arthur and Jane Rickarby, lived in Canterbury, whilst his wife Gladys lived in Appledore, Kent.

Maurice's younger brother, Walter Ashford Rickarby, also served during the war, initially as Private 32721 with the East Surrey Regiment and then as Private 609891 with the Labour Corps. He survived the war and lived to the grand old age of 93 when he passed away on 26 January 1984.

Thursday, 12 September 1918 saw the death of 30-year-old Stoker 1st Class Herbert Ernest **Rogers,** who was serving as part of the crew of HMS *Sarnia* an armed boarding steamer, when he was killed in action when the German submarine *U-65* torpedoed and sunk her in the Mediterranean, off Alexandria. The submarine was under the command of Gustav Sieb.

Herbert has no known grave, but his name is commemorated on the Chatham Naval Memorial. In total, fifty-four of the crew of the HMS *Sarnia* were killed.

His parents, William and Rebecca Rogers, lived in Canterbury.

Thursday, 3 October 1918 saw the death of 27-year-old Private G/2523 H. **Newington** of the 7th Battalion, The Buffs (East Kent Regiment). He was killed in action and buried at the St Sever Cemetery Extension, Rouen, which is situated in the Seine-Maritime region of France.

The Commonwealth War Graves Commission show that his parents, Henry and Alice Newington, lived in Canterbury. which is partly correct. Henry Newington, who was Private H. Newington, was born in January 1891 and at the time of that year's census he was only three months old. His father, also Henry Newington, died at just 24 years of age in May 1891, when Henry junior was only five months old. His mother, Alice Newington, married Henry Wall in August 1895, when Henry was still only 4 years of age. It was decided that he would keep his father's surname rather than changing it to that of his step-father.

At the time of the 1911 census the family home was shown as 2 Railway Terrace, Wincheap Street, Canterbury, by which time Henry and Alice had four children of their own, as well as Henry.

Friday, 4 October 1918 saw the death of 43-year-old Chief Petty Officer 163894 Alfred Albert **Gurney**, who was serving with the Royal Navy as part of the crew of HM *L10*, an L-class submarine, when it was attacked and sunk by German destroyers. She had entered the Heligoland Bight, close to the German mainland and at the mouth of the River Elbe. There she came across a group of five enemy destroyers one of whom, the *S34*, had struck a mine. With all of the vessels close together, HM *L10* had a choice of which destroyer it wanted to attack. The commander of the *L10,* Alfred Edward Whitehouse, manoeuvred his vessel in to position and fired a torpedo into the side of *S33*, which quickly began to sink, but unfortunately the action of firing a torpedo had inadvertently caused the L10's nose to rise to the surface and she was quickly set upon by the remaining German destroyers who then chased her down and sunk her, sending all of her thirty-eight crew to a watery grave.

Alfred's parents, William and Emma Gurney, lived at Westbere, Sturry, Canterbury.

Alfred was the holder of the Naval Long Service and Good Conduct Medal, along with the Africa General Service Medal (Somaliland clasp).

Saturday, 12 October 1918 saw the death of 29-year-old Second Lieutenant Robert Hugh Alban **Cotton**, who died of pneumonia whilst serving with the Army Service Corps. He is buried at the Taranto Town Cemetery Extension, in Italy.

His parents, Charles and Adelaide Cotton, lived in Canterbury.

Monday, 21 October 1918 saw the death of 22-year-old Private S/10519 George Horace **Terry**, of the 2nd Battalion, The Buffs (East Kent Regiment). The fact that he is buried at the Niederzwehren Cemetery in Kassel, which is situated in the Hessen region of Germany, suggests that he was a prisoner of war at the time of his death. The cemetery holds 1,795 graves of Commonwealth service men, many of whom died of their wounds, illness or disease, whilst they were prisoners of war.

There was a camp at Niederzwehren which was begun in December 1914, and mainly catered for British and French prisoners who were captured on the Western Front. Russian prisoners were also incarcerated there and at its peak there were as many as 20,000 prisoners held there. It didn't close until the summer of 1919, which was in keeping with the signing of the Treaty of Versailles at the Paris Peace Conference, on 28 June 1919, which officially marked the end of the First World War.

George's parents, Charles and Harriet Terry, lived at 18 Abbots Place, Canterbury.

Wednesday, 23 October 1918 saw the death of 23-year-old Rifleman 32537 Thomas **Finch**, who was serving with the 5th Battalion, South Lancashire Regiment. He was buried at the Tournai Communal Cemetery Allied Extension, which is situated in the Hainaut region of Belgium.

His mother, Susan Finch, lived at 8 Nunnery Fields.

Saturday, 2 November 1918 saw the death of 20-year-old Private 23/210 Cecil John **Galvin**, who was serving with the 12th Battalion, Durham Light Infantry, when he died of his wounds. He is buried at the Giavera British Cemetery in Arcade, Italy.

His parents, John and Esther Galvin, lived in Canterbury.

Monday, 4 November 1918 saw the death of 20-year-old Second Lieutenant Charles Percival Henry **Manley** of the 8th Battalion, Queen's Own (Royal West Kent Regiment). He died of his wounds and was buried at the Terlincthun British Cemetery, at Wimille.

His parents, the Reverend Charles and Mrs Mary Jane Manley, lived at St Dunstan's Vicarage, Canterbury.

Wednesday, 6 November 1918 saw the death of 21-year-old Private 270372 Sidney Thomas **Pegden**, who was serving with the The Buffs (East

Kent Regiment), when he died of disease. He was buried at the Terlincthun British Cemetery, at Wimille, in the Pas de Calais region of France. He had previously served as a Private (2737) with the 10th Royal East Kent and West Kent Yeomanry Battalion.

His parents, Alfred and Sophia Pegden, lived at 1 Park Lane, Elham, Canterbury. Besides Sidney, they had four other children: sons Alfred and William, along with daughters Ella and Mary.

Wednesday, 6 November 1918 saw the death of 23-year-old Private M2/050876 Leslie Richard John **Yates**, whilst serving with the Reserve Mechanical Transport Company, Army Service Corps. He died of pneumonia and is buried at the Treviso Communal Cemetery, in Italy.

His widow, Mrs Kate Yates, lived at 2 Maida Vale, Island Road, Sturry, Canterbury.

Thursday, 7 November 1918 saw the death of 24-year-old Corporal 445534 Murdoch Robey **Grant**, whilst serving with 1st Battalion, Canadian Infantry (Western Ontario Regiment). As he is buried in the St Mary's churchyard in the village of Kemsing, Kent, he must have died of his wounds, illness or disease, quite possibly whilst a patient at the VAD Auxiliary Hospital that was at Kemsing.

His widow, Ada Florence Grant, lived at 1 Albion Place, Broad Street, Canterbury.

Sunday, 10 November 1918 saw the death of 26-year-old Sergeant 85866 Edward Arthur **Miles** of 'C' Battery, 23rd Brigade, Royal Field Artillery, who died of pneumonia. He was buried at the Sainte Marie Cemetery, Le Havre, which is in the Seine-Maritime region of France.

He was a married man, his widow, Bertha Louisa Miles, lived at Bank Side Cottage, New Street, Ash, near Canterbury.

Canterbury men died throughout the course of 1918, with February being the only month in which none perished.

On **Saturday, 19 January 1918** an interesting ceremony took place at the Alnwick Petty Sessions, which saw Private Hugh Burns awarded the Carnegie Heroes Certificate and £10, which was an awful lot of money at the time. The certificate and the money was in recognition of his heroic and successful endeavours in saving the life of a boy from drowning at Canterbury. On 13 October 1917, Private Burns returned wounded from France and found himself in hospital at Canterbury. The following day he went out for a walk, and while crossing a bridge he saw a group of people, and approaching them he found that a young boy, who appeared unable to swim, had fallen in to the water. Despite being in his heavy army uniform and having one of his arms in a sling, Burns bravely jumped in to the river, located the boy, got him to the river bank saving his life in the process. His heroic actions were brought to the attention of the trustees of the Carnegie Heroes' Fund, Dunfermline, by the Chief Constable of Canterbury.

This was a remarkable feat of bravery by anyone's standards, but the fact that it was achieved by a wounded man with one arm in a sling jumping in to a river, took it to a whole new level.

In late **February 1918** there was a spate of incidents which took place across the East Kent area, including Canterbury, which would have been deemed distasteful at any time, but were even more inexplicable with a war going on. An unknown individual, believed to be a foreigner, was travelling around the county giving poisoned sweets to children. In Canterbury he gave some sweets to three Payne-Smith sisters whom he had engaged in conversation in a local park. They later became sick and were taken to the Kent and Canterbury Hospital for treatment, but thankfully they were allowed home later the same day and suffered no long-term ill effects. The police had no suspects, but took to referring to the individual as a 'scoundrel'. He would appear to have been slightly more than that.

The beginning of **March** saw a somewhat strange incident take place, when a prisoner at Canterbury Prison escaped. The man had several aliases, but the name he was using at the time of his arrest and incarceration was Charles Brooker. No news was heard of the man for two days, but as a result of enquiries made by the aptly named Detective Sergeant Kent, it was discovered that Brooker who was about 45 years of age and had, in fact, enlisted in the Labour Battalion at the West Kent Depot, using one of his many aliases. He had been put down for foreign draft and had he not been captured, he would no doubt have been sent overseas within a couple of days.

He was returned to Canterbury Prison and handed over to the wardens to continue his imprisonment.

On **Wednesday, 6 March 1918** there was a meeting of the Canterbury Town Council, which saw what might be described as a somewhat unusual if not unorthodox suggestion by Councillor McClemens. He proposed that in future, all air raid warnings be aural. This wasn't the first occasion he had made the suggestion. He said that since his previous request for this idea to be implemented 'conditions' had changed somewhat that had not previously been in existence, although he didn't clarify what these new 'conditions' actually were. Councillor McClemens said that it was important for residents to remain indoors during any future air raids. He went on to say that such warnings were now 'universal' and that he did not know a district where aural warnings were not given, other than in the Canterbury Town area of course. The proposal was seconded and supported by Alderman Anderson.

A lengthy discussion then ensued in the course of which several councillors spoke against the idea of the giving of aural warnings for future air raids, but after a vote was taken the proposal was approved with a healthy majority in support of the idea to have aural warnings given of future air raids up to ten o'clock at night, and to have the warnings given by the sounding of bugles, as was already done in Canterbury to sound the 'All Clear'.

That sounds to me like a recipe for disaster, with one part of Canterbury using bugles to warn people of an imminent air raid, yet another part of Canterbury using the exact same instrument to inform people that the air raid was over. The potential for a tragic disaster if ever I heard one.

On the evening of **Tuesday, 23 April 1918** there was a meeting held at the Foresters Hall, for the purpose of inaugurating a branch of the Women's Citizens Association at Canterbury. The mayor presided over the meeting, accompanied by his wife the mayoress. Also present were Miss Helena Normanton, who was the Secretary

NUWW Badge.

of the General Citizenships Committee NUWW, Mrs Gardiner, the wife of Canon Gardiner, who was acting as the Honorary Secretary. Mrs Prentice, the acting chairwoman of the Canterbury Committee, Mrs Bickersteth, President of the local branch of the NUWW, Mrs Maxwell-Spooner, and Mrs C. Turnbull, of the Women's Co-operative Guild.

It was clear to see how serious the intention to set up this association was by those who were in attendance. The mayor of Canterbury said that he had always been sympathetic with the women's movement and believed that women should have a fair say in matters both local and political. Many of them, he said, had as much at stake as the men and a large number of them were taxpayers. With the passing of The Franchise Bill, it gave a large number of women the right, for the first time, to vote in general elections. By his calculations that was somewhere in the region of 6 million women who would have that right, which meant collectively that they were in a very strong position.

He continued his platitudes for the women's cause, with a passion that was unusual for men of position in society to afford to the fairer sex. He advised them to do their best to 'smash up party politics' as the party system in British politics had played the most appalling havoc in English communal life. He in effect accused politicians of being absolutely 'self-seeking and vicious' and individuals who preferred to keep an office in an illegitimate way which benefited themselves, rather than for the benefit of the country and its people. He hoped that the advent of women in to public life would help to bring in the changes that were needed and long overdue.

The proposal for a Women's Association in Canterbury was put forward by Mrs Prentice and seconded by Mrs Turnbull, and a powerful speech by

Queen Mary's Army Auxiliary Corps Nurse.

Mrs Gardiner provided clarity on how they should move forward and the direction they should take, highlighting that the Association would be open to all women, regardless of whether they had the right to vote or not, nor would an individual's social status in society hold any sway, whether that be high or low.

It was clear to see, not only from the desire to start such an association, but by the open support given to them by somebody as influential as the mayor, that effective change for women was here to stay no matter how long it took to fully come to fruition.

An unusual case went before the Canterbury National Service Tribunal on the evening of **Tuesday, 21 May 1918**, one that it could have easily been argued should not have been heard at Canterbury. The reason for this was that the person in question was Mr Thomas Archibald Bowen, of 43 Nunnery Fields, Canterbury, who was the magistrates' clerk at Canterbury. The members of the Tribunal, who were also Justices of the Peace, withdrew while the case was being heard in front of Councillor J.G.B. Stone, Alderman Pope and Mr Spinks. It might not surprise you to know that the application by Mr Bowen requesting that he be given a conditional exemption from having to undergo military training, was granted unanimously by the three-man Tribunal. No surprise there then.

When Thomas Bowen died on 2 February 1940 at the Kent and Canterbury Hospital, he left £10,173 3s 9d, which by today's value would be nearly £400,000, most of which was left to his wife Jessie who he married in February 1921 when he was 41 years of age.

June 1918 saw a report reach the parents of 20-year-old Miss Ethel Francis Mary Parker of 6 East Street, Sturry Road, Canterbury, that she had been killed on 30 May 1918 whilst serving as a member (9048) of the Women's Army Auxiliary Corps, which later became the Queen Mary's Army Auxiliary Corps, at a Red Cross Hospital in France. What made Ethel's death even harder for her family to bear was the fact that the hospital she was working in was many miles behind the frontline trenches, when it was targeted by a German bomber.

In her last letter to her mother, dated 26 May, she explained how the hospital had been bombed every night for three weeks, and that she had had very little rest. It was two o'clock in the morning of 30 May when an aerial torpedo found its mark which resulted in patients and staff being killed, with others wounded. The Commonwealth War Graves Commission website shows that nine members of the Queen Mary's Army Auxiliary Corps, including Ethel Parker, who were killed on 30 May 1918, were buried at the Abbeville Communal Cemetery Extension, along with six soldiers who I am assuming were patients at the same hospital.

Ethel Parker was good at what she did and was well respected and liked by those she worked with. Before the war she had worked for the precentor and Mrs Helmore in The Precincts at Canterbury, and had been a member of the Girls' Friendly Society for many years. Ethel's father, William George Parker, had been in the army before the war, but was transferred to the Army Reserve before the war had begun. He was called up after the outbreak of war and served with a labour battalion.

Tuesday, 2 July 1918 saw the first anniversary of Canterbury's Communal Kitchen in Northgate Street, and to mark the occasion the Mayor and the Mayoress, Doctor and Mrs Bremner, paid a visit to the kitchen and his worship praised the excellent work that was originated by Mrs Robert Gardiner. He spoke of how impressive it was that the kitchen was self-supporting and had been since the beginning of 1918 and that some 3,000 portions of food were provided each week, which was a remarkable achievement. To celebrate the first anniversary of the kitchen, Mrs Gardiner kindly gave all customers a ticket for two free portions of food, not surprisingly there were many local residents who were only too grateful for the gift.

August was an interesting month in Canterbury, because despite the fact that nobody knew the end of the war was a matter of weeks away, life had a strange normality to it. The newspapers were full of meat prices, livestock sales, wheat and corn prices, and properties to purchase or rent. Cars were for sale even though there were not many who could afford them and the availability of petrol was limited at best. Businesses were looking to buy and sell second-hand lots of furniture. People were wanted for all kinds of different jobs. Canterbury Cathedral and the clergy seemed to be constantly in the news, and the sudden and unexpected death of Canterbury's Member of Parliament, Major Bennett-Goldney, and his replacement Mr G.K. Anderson, were hardly off the front pages of the local newspapers. It certainly appeared to be a vibrant time for the city as the war slowly ground to its ultimate conclusion.

September saw a lot of news about the war being reported in the local press. Corporal A. Johnson of Canterbury who was serving with The Buffs (East Kent Regiment) had been awarded the Military Medal for bravery in the Field, whilst Second Lieutenant R.H. Andrews of the Royal Engineers, the eldest son of Mr and Mrs G.F. Andrews of St Paul's, Canterbury, had been promoted to the rank of lieutenant.

Some of the war related news wasn't so positive. News was received of the death of 21-year-old Lieutenant Archibald Francis Hodgskin, who was killed in action whilst fighting against German aircraft, after having carried out a successful bombing raid on a German submarine base on 6 September 1918. His parents, Mr Alfred and Mrs Emily Hodgskin, who lived at 'The Precincts', Canterbury, had two other sons who served during the war. In total they had nine children, five daughters and four sons, one of whom, Harold, enlisted in the Royal Air Force on 23 September 1918 when he was just 17 years of age.

Private G/69670 W.H. Walton of the 4th Battalion, Royal Fusiliers, aged 19 years and 9 months, was killed in action on Wednesday, 21 August 1918, and was buried at the Railway Cutting Cemetery, at Courcelles-le-Comte, which is situated in the Pas de Calais region of France.

Private G/5731 Richard Mannings, of the 2nd Battalion, The Buffs (East Kent Regiment) was 43 years of age and a married man whose widow, Rose Mannings, lived at 6 Wincheap Street, Canterbury. He had initially been reported as having being taken as a prisoner of war by the Germans, but it subsequently turned out that Private Mannings had actually been killed in action on 3 May 1915, more than three years earlier. His body had never been recovered, but his name was commemorated on the Menin Gate Memorial.

What must it have been like for poor Rose, living in what was actually a false belief that her husband was alive, when he had actually been killed, even before she had received the news that he had been captured and taken as a prisoner of war.

Richard had enlisted in the army in April 1915. For the nineteen years before that he had worked for Messrs Williamson's Tannery.

Menin Gate Memorial.

Lance Corporal 207713 William Terry, who was 21 years of age and who served with the 11th Battalion, The Queen's (Royal West Surrey Regiment), was killed in action on Sunday, 18 August 1918. He was buried at the Lijssenthoek Military Cemetery, which is situated in the West-Vlaanderen region of Belgium.

His parents, Charles and Ellen Terry, lived at 18 Abbot's Place, Canterbury.

With the war getting close to its end, **October** saw numerous mayors from around the country giving their views on conditions of peace, at the invitation of a national newspaper. Canterbury's Mayor, Doctor Ramsay Allan Bremner had this to say.

> I think that whatever happens, even if we had to fight the world, we should insist (1) that there shall be no compromise whatever with Germany, and (2) that British supremacy of the seas shall be maintained. Also, under no circumstances must we make peace until every man and woman in Germany who has been brutal to our prisoners has been punished, and guarantees are given for repatriation of all damage, both monetarily and structurally.

The afternoon of **Sunday, 17 November 1918** saw a united service of thanksgiving for victory and the return of peace, which was held in the nave of Canterbury Cathedral. There was a full congregation mainly of dignitaries inside, with massive crowds filling the surrounding streets which created an image that undoubtedly lived in the memory of those who were present forever more.

At about 2.30 pm an imposing procession started from the Cattle Market en route to the cathedral. As on the occasion of Remembrance Day, the marshalling of the procession was in the hands of Mr E.G. Hammond, JP, and Mr H.J. Stone, by whom the work was once again extremely efficiently carried out. Headed by the band of the Northumberland Fusiliers, the long and orderly procession was composed of police officers, members of the Kent and County Fire Brigade, representatives of the Girl Guides, the Church Lads brigade, under Captain C.A. Gardner, Boy Scouts of the 2nd and 3rd Canterbury troops, under Scoutmasters Mr S. Haynes and Mr F. Wood, cadets of the Simon Langton Boys' School under Lieutenant Hall, members of the Women's Auxiliary Army Corps, Voluntary Aid Detachment members under Lieutenant Holgate-Smith, representatives from St John Ambulance Brigade, the RAF, along with the mayor, the County Sheriff, local magistrates and other local officials and dignitaries.

Among other processions to the cathedral was the imposing one of the military under the command of Major-General Dallas and his staff. Men of the Kent Volunteer Force, under Captain C. Terry, and the Motor Transport Section under Captain G.R. Barrett.

It was a truly fitting occasion to commemorate those from the city of Canterbury who had served their nation in its hour of need, and to those on the home front who had carried out voluntary work, whether as a member of a VAD, or the Kent Volunteer Force. To the men and women who had been much-needed munitions workers, making the very shells which helped win the war. To all those men and women who served their country as part of His Majesty's armed forces, and last but by no means least, to those who were killed and wounded during the nearly four and a half years of bloody fighting.

Although the service was also to celebrate the victory over a tyrannical enemy who had sought to enslave all Allied nations, there was also a comprehension by most that, at the time it was only an Armistice that had been signed and that the final details of the end of the war still had to be agreed, but for the time being the fact that they were experiencing the best 17 November since 1913, would suffice.

CHAPTER SIX

1919 – The Aftermath

For many, the end of the First World War would have been a bittersweet moment. People were joyful in the knowledge that the war with all its horrors was finally at an end, but so many had been directly affected by it. Wives had lost husbands, children had lost fathers, parents had lost children, siblings had lost siblings, and the list goes on. One aspect of this scenario which always seems to be forgotten is the effect on those soldiers who survived, a number of whom returned with life-changing injuries. For others it was the sadness of losing friends and colleagues whom, in many cases, they had witnessed the death of. Some had to live with the fact that they had taken another human life, which might be easy for me to write and you to read, but most of these would have been God-fearing men who before the war had been regular weekly church goers; one of the Ten Commandments being 'thou shalt not kill'. They had to try to reconcile their religious beliefs with what they had done, and had to do, just to survive. For many, the only way to do this was to try to block it out and never speak of it again, but regardless of this many were changed men. Thankfully there were many men with Canterbury connections who survived the war, and made it back home to their loved ones physically, at least, unscathed.

With the war over and men once again back in the civilian world, they needed work so that they could provide for their families. Having served their king and country, a job was arguably the least they could expect for their wartime endeavours.

Sadly, once the Armistice was signed and the fighting was over, the death toll didn't come to an end. The following is a list of some of the men with Canterbury connections, who died of their wounds, illness or disease after 11 November 1918.

Second Lieutenant Thomas **Danes**, who was 40 years of age, was serving with the Royal Army Service Corps when he died of pneumonia following a bout of shell shock, on Wednesday, 13 November 1918. He is buried at the Canford Cemetery in Bristol, no doubt because he died in one of the local hospitals.

Faces of the War.

His wife, Beatrice Frances Danes, lived at 'The Pynes', Canterbury.

Lieutenant Colonel Lindsay Buchanan **Scott**, was 54 years of age and was serving with the 1st Battalion, Staffordshire Regiment, but attached to the Army Ordnance Department, when he died of pneumonia on Thursday, 14 November 1918 whilst serving in France. He is buried at the Sainte Marie Cemetery, at Le Havre, in the Seine-Maritime region of France.

His wife, Mrs S.M. Scott, lived at 'Ormdale Lodge', Elham, Canterbury.

Private 87466 Charles Gilbert **Gifford**, was born in Canterbury in 1891. During the First World War he served with the Royal Army Medical Corps at the 11th General Hospital, which was located at Genoa in Italy, and where he died of influenza on Friday, 15 November 1918. He was buried at the Staglieno Cemetery in Genoa.

Sapper 199942 John Henry **Dilnot**, who was born in Canterbury, was 34 years of age and serving with the 7th Field Company, Royal Engineers, when he died of pneumonia on Saturday, 23 November 1918. He was buried at the Cologne Southern Cemetery, which is situated in the Nordrhein-Westfalen region of Germany.

Private L/10212 H **Potter** of the 1st/5th Battalion, The Buffs (East Kent Regiment), who was 23 years of age, died of pneumonia on Friday, 31 January 1919, and was buried at the Mikra British Cemetery, Kalamaria, in Greece.

His parents, Frederick and Susan Potter, lived at 'Longneck House', Waltham, Canterbury.

Lance Corporal 260002 Stanley Walter **Parry** of the 2nd/5th Battalion, The Loyal North Lancashire Regiment, was 20 years of age and born in Canterbury. He died of his wounds on Wednesday, 5 February 1919, and was buried at the Duisans British Cemetery, at Etrun, which is situated in the Pas de Calais region of France.

Private 26475 Albert Henry **Nicholls** of the 10th (Royal East Kent and West Kent Yeomanry) Battalion, The Buffs (East Kent Regiment), was just 19 years of age when he died of appendicitis on Tuesday, 18 February 1919, and was buried at the Ath Communal Cemetery, in the Hainaut region of Belgium.

His parents, Mr W J and Mrs C Nicholls, lived at 40 Black Griffin Lane, Canterbury.

Private 3639 Sydney Cuthbert **Collingwood**, was 28 years of age and born in Canterbury. He was serving with the 51st Battalion, Australian Infantry, Australian Imperial Force, when he died of pneumonia on Saturday, 22 February 1919, and was buried in the St John Churchyard at Sutton Veny, Wiltshire. The No.1 Australian General Hospital, was located at Sutton Veny, which is probably where he was being treated when he died.

Royal Navy Officer's Steward 1st Class 363191 Henry John **Stone** was 35 years of age, when he died of phthisis on Friday, 30 May 1919 and was buried at the Normanston Drive Cemetery in Lowestoft, Suffolk. He was born in Canterbury.

Private 266447 Archie **Price**, was 38 years of age and serving with 1st/1st Kent Cyclist Battalion, when he died of enteric fever on Thursday, 11 September 1919, and was buried at the Delhi Memorial in India.

His widow, Sarah Elizabeth Price, lived at 18 Lancaster Road, Canterbury. His parents, William and Elizabeth Price, also lived in Canterbury.

With the fighting finally at an end, the families of all of these men must have been counting down the days until they saw their loved ones again. Some of them possibly not even aware that their husbands, brothers and fathers, were even ill. How devastating it must have been for them when they discovered that despite surviving the horror and carnage of the First World War, their men folk were never again coming home.

CHAPTER SEVEN

Voluntary Aid Detachment

The work that the Voluntary Aid Detachments carried out was invaluable and without them the welfare of wounded and sick servicemen would have undoubtedly suffered greatly.

I have compiled a list below of the men and women from Canterbury who served with a VAD section during the course of the First World War. It does not include people from outside Canterbury who came to work in one of the town's hospitals. I would have liked to have included more information about each of the individuals, but with more than 700 names included in the list, it would have made the chapter an extremely large one. If you recognise any of the names on the list and want to find out more detailed information about them, then you can do so by searching through www.vad.redcross.org.uk and www.ancestry.co.uk.

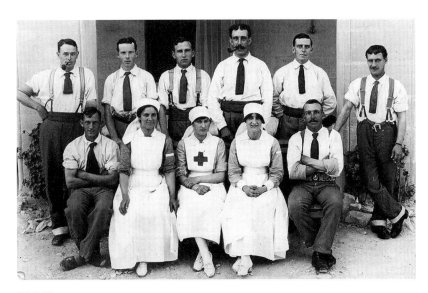

VAD Nurses.

VAD Nurses.

Voluntary Aid Detachments consisted mainly of women, who worked in such roles as auxiliary nurses, cooks, cleaners, or gardeners. Men also worked for the VAD, and were usually employed as drivers, orderlies or stretcher bearers.

Miss Lilian Aglett
Miss Caroline Helena Allardyce
Mr Chester Thomas Amos
Miss Joyce Evelyn Amos
Miss Grace Ashenden
Miss Edith Ashton
Mrs Edith Austin
Miss Ellen Baker
Miss Maud Stackpole Bambridge
Mrs Avis Barrell
Miss Helen Bartholomew
Miss Millie Maud Barwick.
Mrs Mabel Beatson
Miss Dorothy Helen Bellar.
Miss Emily Bennell

Miss Daphne Aitken
Mrs Florence Allen
Miss Doris Gertrude Amos
Mrs Maud Hester Anslow
Miss Mildred Ashenden
Miss Fanny Mason Atkinson
Miss Ethel Aylett
Mrs Ida Baker
Miss Mabel Helen Banks
Miss H.M. Barrington
Miss Mona Katherine Bartlett
Mrs Lilian Bates
Miss Winifred Beatson
Mrs Annie Bellingham
Doctor Arthur Beresford-Jones

Miss Elizabeth Beresford-Jones
Mrs Maud Bigglestone
Miss Florence Ivy Bignell
Miss Lily Bird
Miss Mildred Bishop
Miss Rose Boucher
Mrs Annie Brett
Mrs Lily Brickenden
Mr Robert Holney Brown
Miss Kathleen Bunce
Miss Mona Katherine Bartlett
Miss Mary B.S. Bowen
Miss Emma Bowman
Mrs Florence M.L. Brannan
Miss Winifred Kate Brazi.
Miss Kate Brenchley
Mrs Annie Brett
Miss Julie Broadley
Mrs Constance Annie Browne
Mrs Ethel Kate Burgess
Miss Ethel Carr
Mrs Florence Carter
Mrs Laura Whitley
    Dilnot Chambers
Mrs Mary Charlton
Miss Mabel J. Claydon
Mrs Helen Coleman
Miss Dorothy Collard
Miss Katherine Ada Collard
Miss Ethel Kate Cook
Mrs Alice Mary Cooper
Miss Violet Cork
Miss Hilda Court
Miss Hannah Louisa Cox
Mr Robert Croft
Miss Gladys Crosse
Miss Lucy Mabel Crouch
Miss Mabel Cruttende
Miss Gertrude Davey
Miss Florence Emma Davies
Mrs Florence M. Davis, OBE
Miss Maude De Lasaux.

Miss Margaret Bigge
Miss Minnie Bigglestone
Miss Adelaide Bird
Mrs Eleanor Birley
Mr Reginald Bolton
Doctor Ramsay Allan Bremner
Miss Annie Brett
Miss Julia Broadley
Mrs Constance Annie Browne
Miss Helen Bartholomew
Mrs Blanche Bowen
Miss Annie Bowman
Miss Helen Bracey
Mrs Fannie R.M. Braund
Mrs Dorothy Bremner
Doctor Ramsay Allan Bremner
Mrs Lili Brickenden
Mr Robert Holney Brown
Miss Kathleen Bunce
Mrs Clara Evelyn Buss
Mrs Mary Carson
Miss Nellie Caudle

Mrs Mary Fells Chandler
Mrs H.K. Clarke
Miss Maude Clements
Miss Bessie Collard
Mr Fredrick Collard
Miss Elsie Elizabeth Cook
Mr William Coombs
Miss Violet Cordeaux
Miss Annie Court
Miss Edith Cowell
Miss Violet Cremer
Mrs Phoeby Crosby
Miss Elizabeth E. Crothall
Miss Nellie Crouch
Miss Helen Cunningham
Mr Charles David
Miss Marjorie Davies
Mrs Winnifred Dawson-Scott
Miss Elena de Vial

Mrs Edith Deeks
Miss Mabel Denne
Miss Eleanor Connell Dixon.
Miss Nellie Dobson.
Miss Ethel B. Dowker
Miss Elsie Maud Drayson
Miss Ellen Du Pont Swordes
Miss Mary Dunkin
Miss Mabel Easton
Mr Charles Elam
Miss Bertha Elliot
Miss Ethel Everest
Miss Marjorie Farnol
Miss Betty Ferguson
Miss Blanche Feron
Miss Alice Maria Finn
Mr George Finn
Mrs Daisy Finner
Mrs Lena Fitzgerald
Miss Mabel Flint
Mrs May Foad
Miss Rosie Fowler
Miss Laura Carol Frend
Mrs Mary Camilla Friend
Mr John Charles Galvin
Mis Margot Gardener
Miss Dorothy Gilham
Miss Daisy Goodwin
Miss C. Goulden
Miss Louisa Emily Groombridge
Mrs Bessy Guested
Miss Winifred Haines
Mrs Ethel Hankin
Mrs Agnes Ellen Harris
Mr Leonard Percy Hayward
Mrs Winifred Annie Heard
Miss Maud Eleid Helden-Phillips
Mrs Maggie Hewitt
Mrs Iris Temple Hirst
Mrs Frances Nellic Hodge
Mrs Ruby Holgate-Smith
Mrs Lydia Mary Holman

Miss Kate Denne
Miss Norah Denne
Miss Gladys Dobson
Miss Ellinor Dodds
Miss Doris Dray
Mrs Emily Drayson
Miss Caroline Duckett
Miss Annie Easterbrooke
Miss Joan Eastwood

Mrs Lucy Elizabeth Evans
Miss Jane Hannah Fair
Miss Dorothy Farrier
Doctor Robert James Ferguson
Mrs Louisa Filmer
Miss Cicely Finn
Mrs Jane Finn
Miss Mary Fisher
Miss Edith Lilian Fleury
Mrs Francis Daisy Flood
Mr Edward Foster
Miss Ethel Fox
Miss Nancy Frend
Mrs Katie Simmons Furlong
Mrs Annie Gambell
Mrs Charlotte Gardiner
Mr Gordon Goldfinch
Mrs Alice Mildred Goulden
Mr Walter Green
Miss Gracie Grylls-Watson
Mrs Eva Haggard
Mrs Helen Handford
Miss Constance Harden
Miss Doris Harrison
Mr Albert Head
Miss Dorothy Cecily Jane Hegan
Miss Maggie Hewitt
Miss Kathleen Hilton
Miss Alexandria Hitchins
Miss Lilian Mary Hogben
Mr Frank Holgate-Smith
Mr Herbert Holtum

Miss Alice Homersham
Mr Walter James Hopkins
Miss Dorothy Housyball
Miss Elizabeth Hume
Mrs Kate Hunt
Mrs Clara Grace Jarrett
Miss Lily Johncock
Miss Frances Stephanie Kennett
Miss Florence King
Miss Minnie King
Mrs Marion Kingsford
Miss Lizzy Knight
Miss Charlotte Laing
Miss Mary Sophia Last
Mrs Agnes Mary Le Fevre
Miss Jenny Le Fevre
Miss Amy Leathers
Mrs Jane Ledger
Miss Mabel Frances Mary Leman
Mrs Elizabeth Lent
Miss Kathleen E. Lewis-Barnes
Mr Frederick Link
Miss Edith Luckin
Miss Gertrude Macfarlane
Miss Ellen May Manooch
Miss Helen Marchant
Miss Alex A. Marshall
Mr George Byng Marshall
Miss Mary Martin
Miss Alice Maud Mason
Miss Gertrude Annie Maxted
Miss Maud Maxted
Miss Ethel Medhurst
Mrs L. Mitchell
Mrs Lilian Mable Monger
Mrs Beatrice Mary Robinson
(Was Miss Beatrice Mary Moore)
Miss Ursula Morris
Miss Florence Agneta Mourilyan
Mrs Francis E. Muir
Miss J. Edith Nash
Miss Winifred Newport

Miss Marjorie Honeyball
Miss Dorothy M. Howard
Mr Charles Howes
Miss Dorothy Anne Hunt
Mrs Annie Jacobs
Mr Henry Jenner
Mrs Alice Kennedy
Mrs Gertrude Harriet Kennett
Mrs Leah King
Mr William Andrew King
Miss Alice Kingston
Mrs Hannah Jane Knight
Miss Susan Laing
Captain Frederick Charles Le Fevre
Miss Eliza Le Fevre
Miss Pearson Le Fevre
Miss Doris Ledger

Mr Frederick Bareham Leney
Miss Mary Lester
Miss Edith Liddiard
Mrs Laura Lockie
Miss Evelyn Macfarlane
Miss Jessie Maily
Miss Catherine Maple
Miss Eliza Marsh
Mrs Eliza Marshall
Mrs Margaret Marshall
Mr Thomas Martin
Miss Hilda Mason
Miss Margaret Maxted
Miss Victoria Meason
Miss Catherine Miller
Miss Ethel Kate Moat
Miss E. Moore

Mr Edward Moss
Miss Maude Sarah Mourilyan
Mrs Florence A. Murrell
Miss Kathleen Newman
Miss Marjorie Nicholas

Miss Florence Nightingale
Miss Irene May Oldham
Mr Stanley Ogden
Miss Audrey Patterson
Miss Marjorie Pemberton
Mr Edward Pembry
Miss Nell Penn
Mr Edwin Pepper
Miss Mollie Petley
Miss Stella Gwendoline Pettit
Miss Dorothea Agnes Plumtre
Major General Sir
      Charles Herbert Powell
Miss Fredrica Mary Mantell Pratt
Miss Elsie Elizabeth Press
Mrs Grace Price
Mr Arthur Douglas Ramsey
Mr Edward Douglas
      Whitehead Reid
Miss Catherine Broadwood Rivaz
Mrs Mary Beatrice Robinson
Miss Cecil Russell
Miss Alexandra
      Alberta Russell, MBE
Doctor Samuel Edward
      Thornhill Shann
Mr John G. Sharp
Mrs Lilian Short
Mr Frank Holgate-Smith
Miss Joan Somerville
Mrs Edith Spicer Cowan
Miss Louisa Spinner
Miss Frances Stanford
Mrs Hycinth Staple
Miss Jessie Stead
Mr Edward Stile
Miss Elsie Stroud
Miss Constance Studman
Miss Maud Tassell
Miss Gertrude Taylor
Mrs Hylda Ellen Taylor
Miss Bertha Terry

Mr George Norris
Miss Alice Mary O'Mahoney
Miss Lilian Packham
Miss Florence Jane Pearce
Mr Albert Pembry
Miss Grace Penn
Miss Winnie Pentercost
Miss Dorothy Mary Petley
Miss Dora Markland Pettit
Miss Mabel Pittock
Mrs Fanny Pollard

Mrs Agnes Pratt
Mr Zachariah Prentice
Mr Henry Octavius Preston
Miss Florence May Pye
Miss Judith Rayner

Miss Barbara Rivaz
Miss Nancy Robertson
Miss Ethel May Rolfe
Miss Elsie Agnes Rye

Miss Joan Russell

Mrs Alice Sharp
Miss Ellen Sherwood
Miss Mabel Nightingale Slater
Miss Mabel Beatrice Smith
Miss Irene Gertrude Spanton
Miss Ethel Trix Spinner
Miss Elsie Sprall
Mrs Emily Stanley
Mr Alvis T. Stapley
Miss Edith Annie Steed
Mrs Isabel Strand
Miss Norah Strouts
Miss Mary Suttie
Miss Annie Jane Taylor
Miss Helen Taylor
Mr Ivan Maxwell Taylor
Mr Edwin Terry

Miss Lily Terry
Miss Margaret Thomlinson
Miss Sylvia Thornton
Mrs Gertrude Titmous
Miss Mary Penelope F. Trueman
Miss Lydia Tumber
Mr George Uden
Miss Gertrude Vautier
Mr Harold Wacher
Doctor Sydney Wacher
Miss Elsie Blanche Wake
Mrs Amy Walton
    (Mrs Amy Freeman)
Miss Hilaire Wastall
Miss Annie Watson
Miss Beatrice Watts
Miss Gladys Weatherly
Mrs Bessie Wells
Miss Annie Elizabeth White
Miss Jessie White
Miss Susan Annie Maria White
Mr John Wilford
Miss Gladys Hanree Williams
Miss Mildred Florence Williamson
Miss Muriel Rose Williamson
Mrs Marguerite Rowley Wilson
Miss Kathleen
    Gwendolian Wiltshire
Mr John Worsfold

Mrs Lilian Thomas
Miss Joyce Thompson
Miss Lilian Elizabeth May Tidd
Miss Lillian Townley
Miss Beryl Tuke
Miss Rosa Turmaine
Mr Henry Upton
Mr Sydney Vincent
Miss Joan Wacher
Mrs Violet Wacher
Mr James E. Wales

Miss Marjorie Warren
Miss Ada Watson
Mrs Daisy Watson
Miss Millie Watts
Miss Alice Weeks
Miss Nellie Welsh
Miss Henrietta White
Miss Cissie White
Mrs Mary Ann Widdett
Mr Archibald Wilkins
Mrs Helen Mary Williams
Miss Ethel Wilmore
Miss Stella Marion Wills
Miss Norah Wiltshire

Miss Ethel With

A large number of people on this list carried out the roles that they did voluntarily. The vast majority of them were women and for the married ones amongst them that would have meant balancing their VAD work alongside caring for their family and home, with everything that entailed. These were extraordinary people who didn't just 'do their bit', they did much more, going above and beyond what was required of them, because circumstances dictated they needed to. The majority of them didn't moan about the extra work they were called upon to do, they just got on with it and accepted it as their normal routine.

If I have inadvertently missed anyone off the list, spelt their name incorrectly or allocated them an incorrect pronoun, please accept my apologies and accept that it is down to nothing more sinister than an unfortunate oversight on my part.

VAD Nurses.

CHAPTER EIGHT

Canterbury War Memorial

On one side of the Canterbury War Memorial, is the following inscription.

IN GRATEFUL
COMMEMORATION
OF THE OFFICERS
NON-COMMISSIONED OFFICERS
AND MEN OF CANTERBURY
WHO GAVE THEIR LIVES FOR
GOD, KING AND COUNTRY
IN THE GREAT WAR 1914-1919
THIS MEMORIAL WAS ERECTED
BY THEIR PROUD AND
THANKFUL, FELLOW CITIZENS
"TRUE LOVE BY LIFE
TRUE LOVE BY DEATH IS TRIED
LOVE THOU FOR ENGLAND
WE FOR ENGLAND DIED."
UNVEILED BY
FIELD-MARSHAL THE EARL HAIG
DEDICATED BY
THE ARCHBISHOP OF CANTERBURY
OCTOBER 10TH 1921.

Inside Canterbury Cathedral is a memorial to the officers and men of the 9th Queen's Royal Lancers who were killed in action or died of their wounds or illness, during the course of the First World War. There are the names of 274 men engraved on the memorial, although as with many such memorials it doesn't necessarily include all of those men from the unit who died during the war.

Canterbury War Memorial.

Adkin, W.E.	Adley, E.E.	Allen, E.R.
Amies, N.	Amos, P.G.	Andrews, W.V.
Antram, H.W.	Argrave, A.G.	Argrave, F.
Argarve, F.S	Argrave, G.A.	Argrave, G.P.
Ashman, E.G.	Austen, H.	Austin, C.N.
Austin, H.F.J.	Austin, L.V.	Austin, W.F.
Austin, W.H.	Axten, E.G.	Bailey, F.
Baillie, A.P.	Bainton, H.S.	Baker, A.R.
Baker, E.G.	Baker, W.	Bambridge, B.S.
Banks, J.E.	Barker, A.L.	Barker, C.
Barnes, H.B. (DCM)	Barnett, C.L.	Bartlett, L.A.
Bath, A.H.	Baynes, W.H.	Bean, A.
Beaumont, A.	Benge, F.J.	Benge, W.C.
Bennett-Goldney, F.	Benson, E.T.	Berry, W.W.
Bestow, C.	Bing, E.C.	Bing, E.W.
Birch, F.C.F.	Birch, W.C.	Birch, W.J.
Bowen, G.F.	Branchett, E.E.	Brett, T.
Brickenden, F.	Broadbent, E.T.	Bromley, W.T.
Browning, F.	Browning, J.E.	Bufton, B.
Burden, E.J.	Burnett, J.E.	Burningham, A.
Burrows, T.	Burton, F.W.	Burton, W.E.
Busbridge, L.R.	Bush, A.E.	Bushell, A.J.
Bushell, C.	Bushell, C.N.	Bushell, J.
Butcher, W.C.	Buttery, S.	Carden, E.T.

Carden, G.C.H.

Carden, T.

Carery, T.H.

Carney, T.

Carson, M.

Carswell, P.

Carter, A.

Carter, C.J.

Chambers, C.F.

Chapman, A.

Cheeseman, G.

Clark, C.E.

Clark, G.T.

Clark, G.W.

Clarke, H.

Claydon, B.

Cleaver, S.C.

Clements, C.H.

Colbran, H.

Coley, F.J.

Coley, G.H.

Coley, H.J.

Cook, A.G.

Cook, A.T.K.

Coomes, P.E.

Cooper, S.T.

Coppard, W.J.

Cork, J.

Corrigan, V.M.

Cotton, R.H.A.

Cousens, F.W.

Couter, G.S.

Cowper, W.D.

Cox, W.J.

Cozens, H.S.

Craddock, W.

Crichton, A.R.

Crippen, S.G.

Crisp, A.

Critchlow, E.

Crow, F.G.

Crowther, J.

Cullen, A.J.

Curd, S.P. (MM)

Dann, W.F.C.

Daniel, D.B.

Darby, H.J.T.

Darby, J.

David, C.H.

Davies, H.V.

Davis, B.

Dawkins, J.H.

Dixon, C.G.

Dobson, C.

Dobson, W.T.F.

Doe, F.S.

Downer, A.A.

Drury, W.

Dugdale, G.

Dunk, A.

Dunster, A.L.

Easton, F.

Easton, W.

Edwards, B.J.

Ellis, G.

Ells, G.F.

Elvidge, H.

Escott, R.S.

Fairbrass, H.

Fairbrass, P.J.

Fairbrass, S.

Farmer, E.

Fedarb, T.

Fedard, W.L.

Ferguson, J.A.R.

Filmer, E.F.

Finch, T.

Folwell, P.

Foord, W.

Ford, F.H.

Foster, D.

Fowler, H.J.

Foy, T.E.

Freeman, G.T.

French, A.W.

Furley, B.E.

Furley, W.H.

Galvin, G.J.

Galway, A.E.

Gambell, R.

Gardner, H.F.

Garland, C.

Garrett, W.C.

Gawler, F.

Gawler, R.

Gawler, B.H.

George, E.E.

Gibbs, V.W.

Gibbs, W.E.

Gilbert, W.

Giles, A.

Giles, F.G.

Giles, H.

Gilham, A.T.

Gilham, C.H.

Gill, C.A.

Godden, H.

Goldfinch, J.

Goldsack, A.L.B.T.

Goldsack, A.L.F.D.

Goldsack, E.C.

Gomm, E.A.

Good, H.L.

Good, M.

Goodban, S.L.

Gordine, S.J.

Gower, W.

Grace, P.H.

Green, R.

Gurr, J.M.X.

Hackman, W.H.

Hadden, E.

Goldfarb, C. (MM)

Hadlow, A.J.

Hadlow, C.H.

Hadlow, J.J.W.

Hall, E.R.S.G.
Hardiman, W.
Hare, S.
Hart, B.
Harvey, W.
Henning, R.
Hoare, C.
Hogben, A.J.
Hollands, J.A.
Holman, H.
Holmes, W.A.
Holtum, T.A.
Hooker, P.E.
Hopkins, E.
Howell, J.
Howson, A.E.
Hunt, F.H.
Huxstable, E.W.
Ide, L.G.
Jackson, A.C.
Johnings, W.H.
Johnson, T.
Joyce, H.J.
Keeler, W.P.
Kemp, H.C.
Kennett, G.
Knight, E.F.
Laing, R.
Laming, E.
Lawless, P.
Lemar, D.
Levenson, H.
Long, C.H.
Lord, L.
Lott, J.F.
Luckhurst, C.H.
Mannerings, R.
Marsh, A.E.
Marsh, E.L.
Marshall, F.S.
Martin, J.W.
Maxted, C.B.

Hall, H.
Hardiman, W.C.
Harnden, H.J.
Harvey, F.
Haste, S.
Hewett, P.G.
Hoare, W.R.
Hogben, L.T.
Hollands, S.G.
Holmes, G.E.
Holness, W.A.
Home, W.G.
Hookway, J.A.B.
Hopkins, S.
Howes, H.
Howson, S.
Hurd, C.
Iddenden, E.A.
Ireland, G.
Jarman, F.H.
Johnson, A.W.
Jordan, F.
Judges, F.W.
Kelly, P.T.
Kemp, I.W.
Kennett, G.W.
Knight, J.
Laker, W.
Lawford, P.
Ledger, H.P.
Lemar, F.S.
Linton, F.H.
Loram, T.L.
Lott, B.W.F.
Lott, W.
Lyons, L.A.
Mannock, E. (VC, DSO, MC)
Marsh, C.R.
Marsh, J.
Martin, A.F.
Martin, S.
Maxted, W.J.G.R.

Hannan, V.
Hardman, A.
Harrison, W.
Harvey, P.E.
Henley, F.
Hilder, W.
Hodgskin, A.F.
Holden, P.F.N.
Holliday, A.J.
Holmes, S.A.
Holtum, L.E.
Hooker, E.T.
Hopkins, A.M.
Hopkins, W.
Howland, E.H.
Huggins, A.
Hutton, W.
Iddenden, F.A.
Iverson, H.E.
Jarvis, W.
Johnson, E.F.
Joy, W.B.
Keeler, S.T.
Kemp, A.C.
Kennedy, A.M.
Kennett, S.L.
Laing, C.W.
Lambert, T.J.
Lawless, A.
Legge, A.
Lemar, T.
Lock, L.S.
Lord, A.J.H. (DCM)
Lott, F.
Love, W.
Manley, C.P.H. (MC)
March, A.W.
Marsh, D.S.J.C.
Marsh, R.H.
Martin, C.A.
Martin, W.H.
May, G.V.W.

May, G.

McKinlay, J.

Micklejohn, W.

Millgate, H.

Milton, F.G.

Mount, C.

Muir, T.J.

Nicholls, A.H.

North, A.W.

Nye, H.S.

O'Mahony, E.J.

Overton, H.J.

Page, E.

Paine, C.W.S.

Parker, E.E.

Parren, E.S.

Pay, J.W.

Pearce, W.A.

Pepper, A.H.

Pillow, P.G.

Powell, B.M.

Powell, J.

Preston, O.

Rampley, W.

Read, E.

Reeves, J.E.

Ritchie, A.S.

Rogers, E.R.

Rose, F.H.

Sandy, B.

Sayers, R.C.

Scott, E.E.

Setterfield, F.H.

Shattock, D.L.

Shufflebotham, S.H.

Sims, W.A.

Sladden, E.

Smith, G.

Smith, T.

Smith, W.J.

Spinner, R.W.

Stafford, W.

May, J.R.

McPherson, D.

Millen, B.

Millgate, H.J.

Moore, P.

Moyes, N.G.

Murray, A.

Nicholls, F.

North, C.G.A.

O'Callaghan, J.

Orchard, J.H.

Page, C.A.

Page, F.

Palmer, T.W.

Parker, E.F.M.

Parry, B.

Payne, C.A.

Pembury, G.W.

Perkins, R.E.

Port, H.

Powell, F.R.

Powell, W.J.

Price, A.

Ratcliff, C.D.

Read, S.

Reid, G.

Robertson, J.

Rogers, H.

Rye, R.

Santer, S.

Sayer, S.

Scott, T.H.

Setterfield, L.J.

Shaxted, J.

Silsby, C.J.

Simms, W.J.

Sladden, E.G.

Smith, J.

Smith, W.

Soames, W.

Strand, A.

Standen, F.E.

McKellar, F.

Mepham, F.H.

Miller, R.A.

Mills, A.A.A.

Moss, W.

Muckleston, G.

Newington, H.

Nicholls, F.H.

Nye, E.

Odd, V.

O'Shea I.J.P.

Page, E.

Page, J.

Parker, A.F.

Parker, W.

Parsons, S.

Pearce, A.

Penn, A.G.

Petts, E.H.

Port, W.

Powell, F.W.

Prescott, W.

Ralph, D.

Ratcliff, H.F.

Redmond, T.L.

Reid, W.J.

Robinson, A.

Rogers, W.

Saddleton, S.

Saxby, S.C.

Scamp, A.

Seary, S.G.

Sharp, E.

Shether, A.W.

Sims, E.T.

Sinden, W.F.

Smith, F.J.H.

Smith, R.H.

Smith, W.H.

Spain, T.E.

Strand, A.J.

Stannard, F.T.

Steed, A.E.	Stoddard, E.	Stokes, E.G.
Stringer, G.	Stroud, F.	Stroud, F.R.
Stutely, F.E.E.	Styles, A.F.	Styles, D.O.
Sullivan, D.	Tappenden, W.G.	Tapsell, F.S.
Taylor, A.P.	Taylor, F.G.	Taylor, J.T.
Taylor, W.G.	Taylor, W.J.	Terry, C.G.
Terry, G.H.	Terry, G.W.	Terry, W.
Theoff, W.H.	Thompson, R.C.	Tilley, T.
Tolputt, H.G.	Tomalin, R.A.	Tomlin, H.
Tomkins, F.A.	Tottman, J.	Tupp, H.
Turner, B.H.	Twyman, E.	Twyman, G.W.
Twyman, J.	Twyman, J.J.W.	Uden, A.E.
Uden, F.E.	Uden, G.	Underhill, C.
Underhill, C.F.	Vass, A.	Velvick, J.H.
Wacher, J.S.	Waite, S.R.	Wales, W.
Wales, W.J.J.D.	Walsh, J.	Walton, W.H.
Wanstall, T.	Wanstall, W.J.	Watson, W.E. (DSO)
Weavers, T.J.	Webb, A.	Webb, B.
Whiddett, F.	Whiddett, F.W.	Whiddett, G.H.
Whiddett, J.R.	Whitcombe, S.J.	White, J.C.
Whittingstall, A.E.	Wiffen, E.	Wiffen, W.E
Wilkinson, B.J.	Willey, C.F.	Williams, E.H.
Wilson, A .	Wilson, B.	Wilson, T.
Wilson, W.	Willsden, H.E.	Wimsett, A.H.
Winterhalter, E.	Wood, H.	Wood, J.
Woods, N.A.	Woolmore, D.T.	Wootton, C.
Wraight, A.E.	Wright, H.G.	Wright, W.L.
York, F.A.	Young, F.R.	

The standout name of this list is without question Edward Mannock, who at the time of his death was a major in the Royal Air Force, and one of Britain's most highly decorated wartime individuals. By the time of his untimely death at the age of 31, on 26 July 1918, at Calonne-sur-la-Lys near Pacault, in France, he had already been mentioned in despatches, had been awarded the Distinguished Service Order three times, and the Military Cross twice, before being posthumously awarded the Victoria Cross. At the time of his death he had amassed sixty-one 'kills' of enemy aircraft, which made him the fifth highest scoring pilot of the First World War.

It has to be said that his link with Canterbury is somewhat tenuous, and the question has to be asked whether his name would have actually been included on the list of those commemorated on the Canterbury war memorial, if it hadn't been for his wartime exploits earning him so many medals for his bravery and courage.

St Pauls Church Roll of Honour.

According to the 1901 census, the first one which he appears in, his place of birth is recorded as having been at Battersea in South London, on 24 May 1887, the youngest of three children born to Edward and Julia 'Mannooch'. Edward senior had been a military man and served as a corporal in the British Army, seeing action at the Battle of Tel el-Kebir during the Anglo-Egyptian war in 1882, where British forces were up against a combined Egyptian and Sudanese army. Soon after his return to England, Edward left the army, and moved his young family to Cork, Ireland in 1887. In 1893, at the age of 29, Edward senior re-enlisted in the army with the 5th Dragoon Guards, a cavalry regiment, and he and his family moved to Meerut, in the Indian state of Uttar Pradesh.

At the beginning of the Second Boer War in 1899, Edward senior was sent out to South Africa with his regiment, whilst his family remained in India. It is not exactly clear when, but the family moved again, this time to England, but it was definitely before the census of April 1901, because the family are recorded as living at Stapley Road, Erith, Kent, at that time. Edward senior was 37 years of age, had once again left the army and was working as an engineer's machinist. At this time Edward junior was only 8 years of age.

Edward T. Mannock.

Whilst researching Edward T. Mannock, I have read on more than one occasion that soon after returning to the United Kingdom at about the turn of the twentieth century his father, who was reportedly a drunk, abandoned his wife Florence and their four children, and never returned. Both the 1901 and 1911 census show Edward Alfred Mannock living with Florence and their children at different locations throughout Kent.

Edward left school in about 1908 and began working for the National Telephone Company, but in 1911 he transferred to the company's engineering department, which was situated in Wellingborough, Northamptonshire. Whilst there he joined the Territorial Army and served with the Royal Army Medical Corps, with whom he was promoted to the rank of Sergeant in 1913. It was about this time that he took a keen interest in politics, and was known to be an admirer of Keir Hardie, the founder of the Labour Party, their first leader, and their first ever Member of Parliament.

In February 1914, he quit his job and made his way to Tilbury where he caught a ship to Constantinople in Turkey, where he had secured a job at the Ottoman Telephone Exchange. Although initially at the outbreak of the war, Turkey and the Ottoman Empire remained neutral, in October the same year they allied themselves with Germany to become part of the Central Powers, which led to Edward being interned as an enemy alien. The camp he was placed in was most definitely not a five star hotel and coupled with a lack of regular meals and poor treatment by the guards, he caught dysentery. As his health seriously deteriorated his Turkish captors allowed him to be repatriated back to England, where he arrived in May 1915, a journey which took two months, during which time he contracted malaria.

Despite not being back to full fitness, he once again put on his Royal Army Medical Corps uniform and was assigned to the Corps 3rd Company, 2nd Battalion, of the Home Counties, Field Ambulance Service, but with the war in full swing, he became restless and wanted to take a more active part in the war and requested a transfer to the Royal Engineers, a request which was finally granted in March 1916. However, the old saying 'be careful what you wish for' quickly came back to haunt him as, much to his annoyance, his new colleagues appeared to have even more apathy towards the war than those he had left behind in the Royal Army Medical Corps.

He was intelligent enough to realise that to resign again wouldn't necessarily look good on his CV, so instead he volunteered for the Royal Flying Corps, received a commission as a Second Lieutenant, and began his pilot training on 14 August 1916 at the No. 1 School of Military Aeronautics, at Reading, Berkshire. Before he was let loose on an aircraft he had to learn about aerial gunnery, map reading and 'flight theory' or what today would be known as aerodynamics. Equipped with all of his new found knowledge, he was sent from Reading to the Royal Flying Corps pilot training school at Hendon, which he took to like a fish to water. He qualified as a pilot on 28 November 1916, with his certificate awarded by the Royal Aero Club showing that his pilot's licence was number 3895. From then on his training intensified, moving to Hounslow on 5 December 1916 to train with the No. 19 Training Squadron, and on 1 February 1917 he was sent to Joyce Green Aerodrome in Hornchurch, Essex, where he became part of No.10 Reserve Squadron and underwent advanced training.

It wasn't until 31 March 1917 that he finally arrived in France as part of No. 40 Squadron, near Lens. His first aerial success on 7 May 1917, had an element

Military Cross.

of bitter sweetness attached to it, as it wasn't a German airplane, but an observation balloon. It was another month before he claimed his first 'kill' when he shot down an Albatros D.lll, biplane fighter aircraft.

He was awarded his first Military Cross on 19 July 1917, which he received in Bethune, situated in the Pas de Calais region of France. Just three months later on 18 October, whilst home on leave in England, he was awarded a Bar to his Military Cross, but he was back in France with No. 74 Squadron before the end of November, by which time he had sixteen confirmed, 'kills'. He was awarded the Distinguished Service Order on 9 May 1918, and by the end of the month his tally had risen to forty-one, and by 6 June he had broken through the fifty mark, and had achieved fifty-one victories.

Mannock took command of No. 85 Squadron which was part of the newly formed Royal Air Force, on 18 June 1918, but that didn't stop him from flying operationally, and he reached the sixty mark on 22 July 1918 when he shot down a Fokker D.I.

Four days later he was dead, shot down whilst flying low over German trenches to view the wreckage of a German LVG two seater aircraft, he had claimed as his 61st and last kill. That he was killed that day is not a contentious issue, what happened to his body, however, is. His aircraft caught fire after being hit by ground fighting and crashed to the ground in flames. Some reports claim that his body was found some 250 yards away from the wreckage of his aircraft, but his remains showed no sign of any gunshot wounds. Lieutenant Donald C. Inglis, a New Zealand pilot who was flying alongside him, could shed no light on the situation. Officially, his body was never recovered and therefore he has no known grave, but his name is commemorated on the Royal Flying Corps Memorial to the Missing at the Faubourg d'Amiens Cemetery in Arras. Besides being included on the Canterbury War Memorial, there is also a plaque with his name on it in Canterbury Cathedral, as well as the Wellingborough War Memorial in Northamptonshire.

A year after his death, but only after prolonged lobbying of politicians and senior military personnel by his ex-comrades, Mannock was posthumously awarded the Victoria Cross.

The citations for his Military Cross, Distinguished Service Order, and Victoria Cross citations, are as follows.

Military Cross citation:

For conspicuous gallantry and devotion to duty. In the course of many combats he has driven off a large number of enemy machines, and has forced down three balloons, showing a very fine offensive spirit and great fearlessness in attacking the enemy at close range and low altitudes under heavy fire from the ground.

The above citation appeared in a supplement to the London Gazette on **14 September 1917**.

Distinguished Service Order citation:

Photograph: Distinguished Service Order.

Temporary Second Lieutenant. (Temporary Captain) Edward Mannock, M.C., Royal Engineers, attached. RAF.

For conspicuous gallantry and devotion to duty during recent operations. In seven days, while leading patrols and in general engagements, he destroyed seven enemy machines, bringing his total in all to thirty. His leadership, dash and courage were of the highest order.

The above citation appeared in a supplement to the London Gazette on **16 December 1918**.

Distinguished Service Order citation to First Bar:

Temporary Second Lieutenant (Temporary Captain) Edward Mannock, D.S.O., Royal Engineers, and RAF.

For conspicuous gallantry and devotion to duty. In company with one other scout this officer attacked eight enemy aeroplanes, shooting down one in flames. The next day, when leading his flight, he engaged eight enemy aeroplanes, destroying three himself. The same week he led his patrol against six enemy aeroplanes, shooting down the rear machine, which broke in pieces in the air. The following day he shot down an Albatross two-seater in flames, but later, meeting five scouts, had great difficulty in getting back, his machine being much shot about, but he destroyed one. Two days later, he shot down another two-seater in flames. Eight machines in five days—a fine feat of marksmanship and determination to get to close quarters. As a patrol leader he is unequalled.

The above citation appeared in a supplement to the London Gazette on **16 September 1918**.

Distinguished Service Order citation to Second Bar:

Air Ministry, 3rd August, 1918.

His Majesty the KING has been graciously pleased to confer the undermentioned rewards on Officers of the Royal Air Force, in recognition of gallantry in flying operations against the enemy:

Awarded a Second Bar to The Distinguished Service Order.

Lieutenant (Temporary Captain) Edward Mannock,

D.S.O., M.C. (formerly Royal Engineers).

This officer has now accounted for 48 enemy machines. His success is due to wonderful shooting and a determination to get to close quarters; to attain this he displays most skilful leadership and unfailing courage. These characteristics were markedly shown on a recent occasion when he attacked six hostile scouts, three of which he brought down. Later on the same day he attacked a two-seater, which crashed into a tree.

The above citation appeared in a supplement to the London Gazette on **3 August 1918**. Somewhat strangely, the award of the First Bar to his Distinguished Service Order was made some six weeks later on **16 September 1918**.

Victoria Cross citation:

Victoria Cross

Air Ministry, Hotel Cecil, Strand, W.C.2., 18th July, 1919.

His Majesty the KING has been graciously pleased to approve of the award of the Victoria Cross to the late Captain (acting Major) Edward Mannock, D.S.O., M.C., 85th Squadron Royal Air Force, in recognition of bravery of the first order in Aerial Combat:

'On 17 June 1918, he attacked a Halberstadt machine near Armentieres and destroyed it from a height of 8,000 feet.

On 7 July 1918, near Doulieu, he attacked and destroyed one Fokker (red-bodied) machine, which went vertically into the ground from a height of 1,500 feet. Shortly afterwards he ascended 1,000 feet and attacked another Fokker biplane, firing 60 rounds into it, which produced an immediate spin, resulting, it is believed, in a crash.

On 14 July 1918, near Merville, he attacked and crashed a Fokker from 7,000 feet, and brought a two-seater down damaged.

On 19 July 1918, near Merville, he fired 80 rounds into an Albatross two-seater, which went to the ground in flames.

On 20 July 1918, East of La Bassee, he attacked and crashed an enemy two-seater from a height of 10,000 feet.

About an hour afterwards he attacked at 8,000 feet a Fokker biplane near Steenwercke and drove it down out of control, emitting smoke.

On 22 July 1918, near Armentieres, he destroyed an enemy triplane from a height of 10,000 feet.'

The above citation appeared in a supplement to the London Gazette on **18 July 1918**.

I could not find a citation for the award of the Bar to his Military Cross.

Edward T. Mannock had compiled a list of fifteen air combat rules. Number four on the list said, 'pilots must keep physically fit by exercise and the moderate use of stimulants. It is not clear if this is a reference to alcohol or drugs such as Benzedrine, which although initially developed for medical purposes, were discovered to have a euphoric stimulant effect on those who took the drug.

CHAPTER NINE

In Closing

I hope you have found my offerings about Canterbury in the Great War interesting, even if only in some small way. In writing this book I have tried to provide an overview of the events of the war, year on year, in a comparison to what was happening in Canterbury. Most of the examples I have selected have a military theme running through them, but not all do.

The First World War was an important event not just in British history, but for many other countries across the world. Four empires collapsed as a result of the outcome of the war, the Ottoman Empire, Austro-Hungarian, the German Empire and the Russian. There were an estimated 37 million casualties both military and civilian from all sides. This was split in to 16 million deaths and a further 21 million who were wounded, which included hundreds from Canterbury.

I felt that it was important to show the normal everyday lives that people led, or rather what could be described as normality for those times. The war affected most people, either directly or indirectly, but people still had to get up every morning, mothers had to look after families, men had to go to work and children had to go to school. People became ill and ended up in hospital. Men went to the pub, got drunk, and fought each other for the most ridiculous of reasons. People committed crime, went to court and got sent to prison, whilst others married and brought up families. These events went on in every village, town, and city across the nation, including Canterbury.

If you have any comments or observations to make about this book, hopefully good, but not so good or indifferent are also ok, I can be contacted via my website at www.stephenwynn.co.uk. Where appropriate I will respond to your e-mail. If you have any information concerning any of the individuals I have written about, I will be more than happy to add a piece about them to the site.

Thanks for reading this book.

Sources

Archives

Royal Navy Registers of Seamen's Services, 1848-1939
Army Registers of Soldiers' Effects, 1901-1929
1911 Census of England
The Official French War History (1921)
British Army First World War Medal Rolls Index Cards, 1914-1920

Publications

Bateman, Audrey, *The Magpie Tendency* (1999)
The *Daily Telegraph* newspaper

Websites

www.ancestry.co.uk
www.britishnewspaperarchive.co.uk
www.cwgc.com
www.military.wikia.com
www.wereldoorlog1418.nl.
Wikipedia

About the Author

Stephen is a happily retired police officer having served with Essex Police as a constable for thirty years between 1983 and 2013. He is married to Tanya who is also his best friend. Both his sons, Luke and Ross, were members of the armed forces, collectively serving five tours of Afghanistan between 2008 and 2013. Both were injured on their first tour. This led to Stephen's first book; *Two Sons in a Warzone – Afghanistan: The True Story of a Father's Conflict*, which was published in October 2010. Both of his grandfathers served in and survived the First World War, one with the Royal Irish Rifles, the other in the Mercantile Navy, whilst his father was a member of the Royal Army Ordnance Corps during the Second World War.

Stephen collaborated with one of his writing partners, Ken Porter, on a previous book published in August 2012, *German P.O.W. Camp 266 – Langdon Hills*, which spent six weeks as the number one best-selling book in Waterstones, Basildon between March and April 2013. Steve and Ken collaborated on a further four books in the 'Towns & Cities in the Great War' series by Pen and Sword. Stephen has also written other titles in the same series of books, and in February 2017 his book, *The Surrender of Singapore – Three Years of Hell 1942-45*, was published. This book was then followed in March 2018 by *Against All Odds: Walter Tull the Black Lieutenant*. Stephen has also co-written three crime thrillers which were published between 2010 and 2012, and centre round a fictional detective, named Terry Danvers.

When he is not writing, Tanya and he enjoy the simplicity of walking their three German Shepherd dogs early each morning, at a time when most sensible people are still fast asleep in their beds.

Index

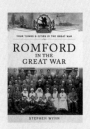
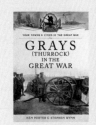

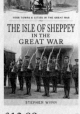

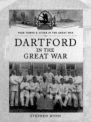

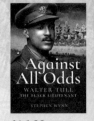